A COMPARATIV
TRAITS OF
AI

Chinal Talesra

CONTENTS

CHAPTER -1
INTRODUCTION

While we try to teach our children all about life, our children teach us what life is all about.

Angela Schwindt

Adolescence is the intermediary stage of development between childhood and adulthood, representing the period of time during which a person experiences a variety of biological and emotional changes therefore this stage can be considered as a middle stage of childhood and adulthood. Every individual passes through this stage. It is a period of physical growth, maturing of mind and behaviors as well. By the end of Adolescence, development reaches a position where an individual is legally and socially regarded as mature, capable of leading an independent life, free from control, supervision and guidance.

An adolescent faces numerous psychosocial challenges during this stage of life. In this period, so many demands are made upon adolescents by society for independence, peer and heterosexual adjustments, educational and vocational preparation and for the development of social and emotional values. Personality development also gets stronger at this stage and continues for a long time. A proper shaping of the personality during this period can prepare a valuable human resource for our nation. Many adolescents face identity crisis in this stage. These psychosocial demands may affect the personality development of an adolescent if one fails to meet them. As John Prine says:

"I'm so mixed up and lonely.

Can't even make friends with my brain.

I'm too young to be where I'm going.

But I'm too old to go back again".

The most commonly used chronologic definition of adolescence includes the ages of 10-18, but may incorporate a span of 9 to 26 years depending on the source **(APA, 2002)**.

According to **Steinberg (2014)** "Adolescence is a dynamically evolving theoretical construct informed through physiologic, psychosocial, temporal and cultural lenses. This critical developmental period is conventionally understood as the years between the onset of puberty and the establishment of social independence".

According to **Chhadva & Kacker (2013)** "Adolescents are unable to understand the emotional turmoil happening within them and thus are unable to tackle effectively emotional pain, conflicts, frustrations and anxieties about the future which are often the driving force for high risk behavior".

Hall, S. (1904) defines "Adolescence as a period of storm and stress to be survived".

This path from childhood to maturity is an attractive, but irregular, insecure and strange. Major mental and physical changes occur in the personality of an adolescent, and he comes into a new world. Adolescence is a time of confusion and curiosity. An adolescent always remains confused whether he is torn between the desire for autonomy and the need to remain dependent on his parents. In this stage an adolescent is also full of curiosity where he tends to be focused on investigating and exploring the world.

Adolescence is the age of rebellious behavior wherein the adolescents might experience problems in adjustment and academic achievement. They may also adapt negative attitudes, disobedience and disrespect. Sometimes they are also found indulged in drug and alcohol abuse and experience peer pressure, depression, stress and issues of sexuality also arises. Television and other media also represent the current issues of adolescents such as gang violence, school shootings, alcohol-related accidents, drug abuse, and suicidal tendency which influence their health and behavior.

Despite the negative picture of adolescents, positive traits can also be seen among them. Most adolescents are social, get success in school and do not experience serious problems such as substance abuse or involvement with violence instead they are actively involved in various creative activities. Adolescents always need the help of adults and want them to be part of their lives. They know that they can look after, teach, guide, and protect them on the path to adulthood.

Stages of Adolescence

There are three stages of adolescence: Early, middle and late adolescence. These changes are accompanied by many changes. Physiological growth, intellectual, psychological and social developmental changes take place during these years to form one's own identity and to prepare for adulthood.

(i) Early Adolescence

Early adolescence usually begins from puberty that occurs from ages 10 to 14. In this stage, rapid bodily changes take place and people start to worry about these changes. They might experience shyness, modesty, and possess a greater interest in privacy. Early adolescents may feel invincible and start to engage in behaviors such as smoking and alcohol use. This period is also characterized by sexual curiosity. Relationships with close friends become more important than family relationships.

(ii) Middle Adolescence

Middle adolescence begins from the age of 15 and ends by 17. Puberty has completed in this stage. Teens in this stage are highly concerned with their beauty and physical appearance. Large amount of their time is spent in thinking about how they look and modifying their appearance.

Relationships orientation changes during middle adolescence. In this stage adolescent's attraction shift from parents to peers. They also worry about sexual attractiveness. Middle adolescents complain about their parents that they prevent them from becoming independent, and they withdraw from them. They may try to assert their independence by refusing to bathe, not cleaning their rooms, and picking up annoying habits. Risk taking behaviors such as alcohol consumption, smoking, drug abusing are significantly increased during this stage.

(iii) Late Adolescence

Late adolescence broadly falls between the ages of 15 and 19. The major physical changes occur during this stage. The brain continues to develop and reorganize itself, and the capacity for analytical thought is greatly enhanced. Peer-group opinions are considered to be important at the outset, but it diminishes as adolescents gain more clarity and confidence in their own identity and opinions. Risk-taking behavior declines during late adolescence, as the ability to evaluate risk and make conscious decisions develops in this stage.

Girls in late adolescence tend to be at greater risk than boys and these risks are often magnified by gender-based discrimination and abuse. Girls are prone to eating disorders as they are concerned about their body image that is fuelled by cultural and media stereotypes of feminine beauty. Late adolescence is a time of opportunity, idealism and promise. It is in these years that adolescents make their way into the world of work or further education, settle on their own identity and world view and start to engage actively in shaping the world around them.

Changes during adolescence

(i) Physical changes:

Adolescence is generally considered to begin with onset of puberty, the process that leads to sexual maturity, the physical changes in both primary sex characteristics and secondary sex characteristics that occurs in the body as sexual development **(Ciccarelli and White, 2015)**. In this stage many glandular changes take place. The thyroid gland increases the rate of growth and the adrenal gland and sex glands stimulate the growth of characteristics such as body hairs, muscle tissues etc in males.

(ii) Cognitive changes

Cognitive development is covert in nature as it cannot be seen directly whereas we can see the physical development but still this cognitive development represents the major change in the way adolescents' think about themselves and the world around them. Adolescents do not care about the feelings of others. This adolescent egocentrism emerges in two ways ie personal fable and the imagery audience **(Ciccarelli and White, 2015)**. In the personal fable adolescents pay out so much time thinking about their own thoughts and feelings that they become influenced that they are special and one of a kind. Therefore it can be said that sometimes personal fable may be dangerous because they feel unique, teenagers may feel that they are somehow protected from the danger of the world and so do not take precautions that they should. This may result in so many risky behaviors such as injury or death while racing in a car, drinking and driving, involving in unsafe sexual activities. In imagery audience, the adolescents become highly self conscious because they think that they are the center of everyone else's. Adolescents also develop stronger reasoning skills, logical and moral thinking, and become more capable of abstract thinking and making rational judgments.

(iii) Psychosocial changes

In adolescents many psychosocial changes also take place. Adolescence is mainly marked by the search for a consistent sense of self. According to Erikson (1950) the psychosocial crisis of identity versus role confusion occurs in this stage and it must be resolved timely. Moreover parent-teen conflict is also a major issue of this stage. Adolescents are more able to take other people's perspectives into consideration and often want to do something about the social issues that they encounter in their lives. Also, adolescents need greater independence and responsibility and they want to take decisions on their own. They don't want parental control in their emotions and actions. Their social and cultural environment affects how adolescents express this desire for autonomy.

(iv) Emotional changes

Emotional changes such as mood swings, movement of adolescents from relationship with family members to society members outside the family; short temperedness, aggression etc are also observed during this stage.

Needs of Adolescents

The period of adolescence is the most critical period of life due to various physical and emotional changes. So adolescents face various problems arising out of certain basic needs. The following are some of the basic needs of adolescents.

1. **Need of freedom from dependence:** Adolescents tend to behave as full-fledged adults. So they do not want to be under the control of elders. Hence, they need freedom and want to exercise their own opinion. This creates difficulties.

2. **Need of association with the opposite sex:** During adolescence, sex instinct attains maturity and is very vigorous. Adolescents adorn their bodies to attract the opposite sex. They feel the need of association with the opposite sex.

3. **Need for self-support:** Self-support implies what adolescents want to become in life. So this need can be fulfilled by providing them educational and vocational support.

4. **Need for philosophy of life:** Adolescents consider themselves as mentally mature and assume independent outlook for every activity of their life. They start taking interest in the matters of religion, talking about conduct and destiny.

5. **Need for Security:** Adolescents lose support of their parents and sometimes also suffer from complexes and frustrations if they are not given sympathetic attitude and guidance.

6. **Need for self-recognition:** Adolescence is a stage of self-decoration and becoming self-conscious. They desire to attract the attention of others. They also want to display themselves in every activity as they need self-recognition. They want to be recognized as full-fledged individuals.

7. **Need for success:** Every adolescent has the desire to succeed in all the activities he undertakes as failure may disintegrate his personality. In contrast if they achieve success, they learn to adjust in a better way.

8. **Need for better food:** The adolescence is a stage of growth and development. The major physical changes take place during this stage. The body develops in height, weight and every other aspect. Therefore, adolescents need rich diet in proper quantity and quality.

9. **Desire for new experience:** The adolescent is never interested in same routine. He is always eager to learn new and new experiences so that he can explore the world around him.

Factors affecting adolescence:

The following factors affect adolescence.

1. Generation Gap:

Effect of generation gap can be seen during adolescence. The adolescent starts living in the company of peers, representing a changing society. He is still not matured enough to have developed his own personality to assert his views or attitudes. The adults always ignore the ideas and views of the adolescents, which results in a constant struggle between an established society and the adolescents.

He remains in a state of tension to have his own way in regard to the fashion, the hair-style, and the ways of talking and in behaving. This way a generation gap is apparently perceivable in the clash between the adolescents and the recognized society of the adults. In some cases, the adolescents consider that the knowledge and skills of the adult generation have become outdated and they lack skills in the use of new technologies. Generation gap, because of this reason aggravates problems for the adolescents.

2. Emotional Instability:

The stage of adolescence may also be a period of difficulties due to emotional instability. An adolescent seems to be very emotional; very sensitive. Sometimes, he also gets nervous through the ebbs and flows of emotions. Lack of patience and tolerance is witnessed in his behavior. During this stage an adolescent passes through physical, mental and emotional development. Due to rapid physical changes, fast growing mental abilities and self-consciousness an adolescent may face difficulty in adjustment. On one side the adult generation expects them to take on new responsibilities, while at the same time, he is not considered mature enough to be entrusted with the same.

The adolescent gets angry, becomes jittery because of physical changes, especially due to menstruation or ejaculation. All this makes the adolescent prone to anxiety. He is cognitively very much developed, can better understand the situations, is more conscious of problems, and, is mature enough to think for his career. In spite of the fact that the adolescence is considered to be a period of development in all fields, emotionally, he becomes unstable, rash, and sometimes reckless.

3. Career- consciousness

As adolescent proceeds towards adulthood, he starts worrying about his career. He starts thinking about the selection of courses and subjects. The adolescent attains the adult level of cognitive development before he is actually grown into adult. Due to this development, an adolescent understands where the best opportunities for his bright career lie; and how he should prepare himself for building up such career. Sometimes, the adolescent fail to attain that level of career- consciousness, and, the fact makes the parents nervous; they start pushing their children to work hard regularly for the desired career. The situation may also cause tension for the adolescent.

4. Socialization:

The growing adolescents should get a very suitable social milieu for the better cognitive and moral development. Adolescence is the period when his attraction shift from parents to peer group. First, his peerage remains confined to his class- fellows; then he crosses the boundary of his class and makes friendship with many of his school-mates. They come in contact with one another while indulging in curricular and co-curricular activities such as sports, scouting, outing, tours and picnic etc. An adolescent becomes keenly interested in spending time with his companions which help in making him very much social and, the environments provided by these different social circles, help in his multi-faceted development.

Importance of Adolescence:

Adolescence is a very important period as both the immediate and long-term effects on attitudes and behavior take place during this stage. This stage involves physical and psychological effects accompanied by mental development. New attitudes, values and interests are also developed during this stage. Adolescent's life is full of hopes, learning new experiences, to find new relationships, to examine and explore their inner strengths. Adolescents need freedom to think and set their own goals and discover different ways to achieve them. Adolescence is a period when boys and girls feel the joy and pride of growing up. However, there are many restraints from home and society that keep them under control. They want adolescents to behave in a right manner and obey the rules at home and outside. Adolescents interact with the external environment and develop their own potentialities. As teenagers get older they become more confident of themselves and are ready to experiment with different roles until they find one that fits them. They are often idealistic and willing to actively practice an issue that's important to them. As adolescents look towards the future and broaden their view of the world. They emerge as a separate entity from their parents and understand their parents' limitations. Until adolescence, a child usually fulfills the will of his parents. But as he matures, he naturally separates from his parents and develops his own distinct personality. Adolescents grow physically, emotionally, and intellectually, develop moral understanding and an ability to plan towards the future.

Birth Order

Birth order is a topic that receives a great deal of attention both in the academic circles, as well as the media and society. Whether being an only child or the youngest of eight, everyone has an ordinal position they identify with and it often becomes a personal label. The birth order labeling begins at a very young age as parents, family members and other adults in a child's life start to refer to the child as such.

Birth order means the ordinal position of birth the child holds in the family. Adler (1927) was the first who explored the concept of birth order in his theory of personality in order to assess the lifestyle of the individual.

Birth order has been defined by **Shulman and Mosak (1977)** as "Ordinal position which refers to the actual birth order of the siblings; as well as the psychological positions, which refers to the role child adopts in his or her interaction with other members of the family".

Sulloway (1996), in his book "Born to Rebel" stated this concept within the framework of evolutionary theory. According to him, siblings rival for physical, emotional and intellectual resources from parents and it causes long lasting differences among siblings which is true across the cultures and throughout history. While siblings use different strategies for getting parental favors; parental responses can also affect the influence of birth order on personality.

The reduction in average annual rate of population growth, which is a global phenomenon, has primarily occurred due to reductions in fertility levels. Due to declining fertility rates and increasing age at first birth in most of the countries in the world, family size is reducing. Fertility decline has brought change in the structure and functions of the family institution. Fertility decline is due to the combined effect of substantial socio-economic development achieved during the last two decades and the effective implementation of family planning programmes. The contribution of socioeconomic development to fertility decline was mainly due to an increase in the cost of children. It became irrational for many people to have large families. It is expected that in the foreseeable future, fertility will remain low and small families will become an acceptable option. Now-a-days, even family with only one child is emerging as a viable alternative life style.

Single-child families have always been there throughout ages, but their number was rather limited. Infertility of either of the spouse was the main reason for it. Earlier, for a majority of people, one child norm appeared to be too fanatical and it was not a family of choice. The proportion of single child families has increased manifold in last two decades. Although there is no database to point out its incidence, yet review of literature highlights that it is an emerging trend especially among the educated upper and middle sections of the society. In urban areas, the individualistic and materialistic values seem to have accelerated this trend. Relationships are viewed through costs, rewards, profits, margins, mergers, and acquisitions. The ascendancy of individualism means that relationships are justified in terms of individual well being and are defined according to individual preferences. The growth of feminism has also prompted women to avoid dependent relationships, and consequently they are taking more time to establish their independence and acquiring motherhood.

All these values have directly affected the relations within family, especially the parent-child relationship. Now-a-days, couples are viewing parenthood as a huge liability and they are not ready to give up their materialistic gains for large family size. They consider large family size a hurdle in acquiring materialistic acquisitions. As a result, fertility levels are declining very fast in urban areas. Urbanization and modernization have replaced high level fertility of pre-modern societies to low-level fertility in the contemporary societies. It has been found that the sections of the society which are most engaged in urbanized and individualistic civilizations have the lowest birth rates.

Both men and women around the world are spending a lot of time in getting education, climbing career ladders and securing their careers. As a result, they are entering late in marital ties or are postponing parenthood. In many countries in Asia where significant declines in fertility are being experienced, reductions in the proportion of married people have often coincided with or preceded declines in marital fertility. A substantial increase in the proportions of never married males and females has been noticed in many countries. This has been facilitated by birth control revolution which has made procreation optional. Even after begetting a child, parents want to provide him the best of the care, education and other pleasures of life. In other words, a strong trade off is going on between child quality and quantity. These notions are strongly influencing the fertility decisions of the couples and encouraging them to limit their family size to only one child voluntarily. This is happening in spite of the societal bias against this family size.

Some other aspects of the urban life that are encouraging this family size, are tremendous work-related stress, long working hours, fast pace of life, little time for intimacy, increase in sexually transmitted diseases and obesity. All these factors are not only affecting the marital relations but also the reproductive capacities of an individual. Along with these, poor nutrition and environmental pollution involved in urban lifestyle is also affecting fertility, resulting in the emergence of involuntary single-child families.

No doubt, single-child families are growing all over the world but due to paucity of authenticated data, it is difficult to assign the causes thereof. The emergence of single-child families has not only influenced the definition and structure of family and kinship network but has also penetrated the socio economic and demographic composition of the society. The research on single-child family being in an infant stage, leaves many unanswered questions viz. whether the single-child families will help in solving the population problem or will it create a dearth of kinship network and life partners for the child due to depleting sex ratio or will it result in some other repercussion for the parents like old age insecurity and dependency on the child, etc.

Single Child

Different terms have been used interchangeably for this family size like one child family, single-child family and only-child family. Single-children have been sometimes categorized as first born, or as last born. They are called by different names like singletons or only borns.

An only child is a personality having no siblings, either biological or adopted.

According to **Falbo (1987)**, "single-child family includes a couple or a single parent who have only one child in their lifetime".

Kusumlata (1987) has defined "single-child family as one in which a conjugating couple has one surviving child".

Breton and Prioux (2009) have stated that "man and woman having only one child during their reproductive life, is a single-child family".

Gillespie (1999) has distinguished between voluntary and involuntary single child families i.e. having this family size by choice or circumstances. The couple who intend to have one child from the outset and fulfill their intention could be said to have made an active decision to have one child 'by choice'. In contrast, the couple who initially intend to have two children but then are unable to have a second due to infertility could be said to have one child 'due to circumstance'.

Throughout history, only children were relatively uncommon. Over the 20th century in particular, birth rates and average family sizes fell sharply, for a number of reasons including availability of birth control and increased formal employment of women. This reduction in birth rates included a larger proportion of one child families.

The only child receives the entire social, emotional, and material resources those parents have to provide. He is their sole beneficiary. Parents invest a great deal of efforts in nurturing and providing for the child and they often have a high expectation of return. They expect the child to turn out well. The only child has unrivalled access to parents and everything they provide. As the only child has no siblings with whom he can connect, to be compared to, to compete against, or to do conflict with, the child becomes adultized from interacting with these primary parental companions.

The only child is sometimes more advantageous than children who have siblings. Singletons sometimes show high school performance, high achievement motivation, higher self esteem and higher abilities, psychological and behavioral adjustment than siblings. Singletons are more prevalent in China due to the Chinese government's enforcement of one-child policy.

Sibling

According to **Mersky Leger and Jane (1993)** "A sibling is one of two or more individuals having one or both parents in common". A female sibling is known as sister and a male sibling is known as brother. In most societies, siblings usually grow up together to develop strong emotional bonds such as love, or thoughtfulness. The emotional relationship between siblings is greatly influenced by parental treatment, birth order, personality, and personal experiences inside and outside the family. Brothers or sisters can be a source of companionship, help or emotional support. Older siblings serve as caretakers, teachers or models; in some situations they can even help compensate for absent or distant parents. In their interactions with each other, siblings acquire many social and cognitive skills which lead to healthy social development. +

Difference between an Only Child and having Siblings:

There are many people we meet in our life who come from different country, culture, and family. We all grow in different environment. For instance, some adolescents are raised as an only child and some are raised along with their siblings. There is a huge difference between being raised alone and raised with siblings. Only child and siblings differ in terms of sharing stuffs. Only child doesn't like to share anything with anyone. On the other hand, siblings like to share things with others. Another difference between being only raised and having siblings is relationship with their family. Siblings always have companions and playmates. They can play together, learn together, have conversation, and share their problems with one another. Also, they can learn from their elder siblings or teach their younger ones. They also help to take care of each other. The older sibling can help the younger sibling to learn how to live with the other, help with homework, etc. In contrary, an only child who receives more attention from his parents, which might give them an advantage over their siblings with completing homework, more time to spend with mom or dad, and perhaps more or better toys, clothes, etc.

In the last decades there has been a continuous diminishing in the mean size of families, a change in the family structure and an increase in the frequency of families with only one child. The absence of siblings and the closeness with adults may interfere in the intellectual and personality development. Some people also believe that only-children receive excessive attention, mature precociously and, due to the absence of siblings, become selfish, demanding, dependent and moody, in comparison to children with siblings. Only-children tend to show traits similar to first-children and seem to have higher self-esteem than children with siblings. However, there are little available data comparing characteristics associated with the condition of being an only-child to the condition of being the first-child and to that of having siblings.

Children have different social interactions in the family depending on their birth order. The first born has little interaction with other children during his early years particularly if he lives in nuclear family system whereas, later born has siblings around him when he joins the family, which allows him numerous interactions with children.

Some people believe that children of a family behave differently although they were raised in the same environment, such as neighborhood, and share the same genetic pools from both of their parents. On top of behaviors, siblings do differ in terms of personality characteristics, intelligence, familial sentiment and others. Firstborns are always described as being responsible, high achievers and perfectionists whereas lastborns and only child are always described as the baby of the house and are mostly spoiled kids.

Generally, parents are excited about their first child and pay more attention, investment, as well as expectation on this child. As the second child arrives in the family, the firstborn may experience dethronement and the same happens to the second born once a third child arrives and so forth. Therefore, every child experiences different level of parental resources and investment which help in shaping their developmental course.

Socio-Economic status

Socioeconomic status is an economic and sociological combined total measure of a person's work experience and of an individual's or family's economic and social position in relation to others, based on income, education, and occupation. In other words, socioeconomic status indicates one's access to collectively desired resources, be they material goods, money, power, friendship networks, healthcare, leisure time, or educational opportunities. It is an easy access to such resources that enable individuals to prosper in the social world.

Socio Economic-Status of a person refers to status of his family in relation to their level of socio-cultural participation, ability to influence mass, level of education, kind of occupation, financial position, health–wellbeing, and lifestyle, level of aspiration, kind of gadgets, services and leisure facilities that the family enjoys. It indicates the social standing or class of an individual. Furthermore, an examination of socioeconomic status as a gradient or continuous variable reveals inequities in access to and distribution of resources.

A social status is an indication of one's position of respect, prestige and influence in the social structure apart from his personal attributes. Socio Economic status means ranking of an individual by the society he lives in terms of his material belongings and cultural possessions along with the degree of respect, power and influence. Socio economic status is based on income, education level, occupational level and social status in the community.

Socio economic status refers to ranking of an individual by the society he lives in terms of his material belongings and cultural possessions along with the degree of respect, power and influence. Socioeconomic status has long been known as a good predictor of academic achievement. Many researchers have demonstrated the importance of the relationship between family background and student achievement. Many studies were conducted in relationship of socio economic status and academic achievement. Students come from very different socio-economic classes, values, intelligence, capacity, ideas; ambitions of the students vary according to their socio-economic status. The factor of status has impact on the academic achievement of the students.

Home background also influences academic and educational success of students. Families with high socioeconomic status provide better facilities for the all round development to their children as they have easy access to wide range of resources. They also impart high quality care, books and toys to encourage them in various learning activities. The parents of high socio economic status can easily get information regarding their children's health, as well as their emotional, social and cognitive development.

Personality

Every human being possesses his own individual personality whether he is a child, an adolescent or an adult. The personality covers a broad range of traits of an individual. Personality is the combination of characteristics that constitute an individual's distinctive character. Personality means individuals' characteristic patterns of thought, emotion and behavior together with the psychological mechanisms. Personality can be defined as consistency in a person's way of being i.e. long term consistency in their particular ways of perceiving, thinking, acting and reacting as a person.

The term personality is used in various senses. Usually, it is used to indicate the external outlook of an individual. In philosophy it describes the internal quality, but in social psychology personality neither describes the external pattern nor the internal quality. It means an integrated whole.

The historical root of the term personality is in the Latin word "Persona" - The mask worn by the Greek actors was called persona. Personality in that sense means a cover for the real person behind it.

According to **Ogden, R.M (1926)** "Personality is the expression of man's inner life and character is the expression of what he does or achieve"**.**

Watson, J. W. (1930) defines Personality as: "Personality is the sum of activities that can be discovered by actual observation over a long enough period of time to give reliable information".

According to **Mc Douglas, J.W (1932)** "Personality is a systemic unit of all mental features in their interplay".

In the words of **Eysenck, H.J (1947)** "Personality is the more or less stable enduring organization of person's character, temperaments, intellect and physique, which determine his unique adjustment to the environment".

According to **All port, G. B (1948)** "Personality is a dynamic organization within the individual of those psycho physical systems that determine his unique adjustment to his environment".

Cattell, R.B. (1967) defines Personality as: "Personality is that which permits a prediction of what a person will do in a given situation".

According to **Larsen & Buss(2005)** " Personality is the set of psychological traits and mechanisms within the individual that are organized and relatively enduring and that influence his or her interactions with, and adaptations to, the intrapsychic, physical, and social environments".

According to **Funder (2004)** "Personality refers to an individual's characteristic patterns of thought, emotion, and behavior, together with the psychological mechanisms – hidden or not – behind those patterns".

Mayer (2007) defines Personality as: "Personality is the organized, developing system within the individual that represents the collective action of that individual's major psychological subsystems".

According to **Pervin, Cervone & John (2005)** "Personality refers to those characteristics of the person that account for consistent patterns of feelings, thinking, and behaving".

In a layman's language personality refers to the personal qualities and characteristics of an individual. Personality describes how we interact with others. It is a sum of characteristics of an individual which distinguish him from the others. It is our personality which makes us unique and helps us stand apart from the mass.

On the basis of above definitions it may be said that there are two main approaches of personality: (a) the psychological and (b) the sociological. According to the psychological approach personality is a certain style peculiar to the individual. This style is determined by peculiar organization of mental trends, complexes, emotions and sentiments. The sociological approach considers personality in terms of status and role of an individual in the group of which he is a member.

Thus, we can say that personality is the sum of the ideas, attitudes, values and behavior of a person which determine his role in society and form an integral part of his character. Every individual has his own characteristic way of behaving, perceiving things and looking at the world. There is no similarity between two individuals. What an individual observes in his childhood days, how he is raised plays an important role in shaping his personality.

Personality is nothing but the aggregate accumulation of memories and incidents in an individual's entire life span. An individual's personality is also affected by environmental and genetic factors, family background, financial conditions etc. If an adolescent has a troubled childhood, he would not open up easily in front of others. Some kind of fear would always be there inside him.

An adolescent who never had any major problems in his childhood would be an extrovert and never have issues interacting and socializing with others whereas those adolescents who were not allowed to go out of home, play and freak out with friends would be introvert and they start believing that their home is their only world and they are not safe outside. Such a state of mind soon becomes their personality.

Characteristics of Personality:

1. Personality is unique in each individual. It is not possible for any individual to imitate the qualities of the personality of other individual.

2. Personality refers to determined qualities of an individual. Every individual has some traits and qualities and they try to adjust with the environment.

3. Personality represents an active direction of an organism to environment. Personality is a continuous process of learning and all the traits of personality are not acquired at once.

4. Personality is influenced by social interactions. Personality is a result of social-interaction, not an individual quality. When we interact with other members of the society, we acquire some qualities while we exhibit certain others. This constitutes our personality.

Determinants of Personality

The following factors influence one's personality.

(I) Heredity

Heredity influences the personality in the following ways.

(a) Constitutional Factors

This is an effective factor in determining the type of Personality. We are always impressed by an individual who has a muscular and a well proportioned personality. Height, Weight, physical defects, health and strength are the main factors which affect our personality.

(b) Biological Factors

Biological factors also affect an individual's personality. The functioning of the nervous system, glands and blood chemistry determines our characteristics and habitual modes of behavior. These factors form the biological basis of our personality.

(c) Intelligence

Intelligence also affects an individual's personality. Persons who are very intelligent show better adjustment in home, school and society than those who are less intelligent.

(d) Sex Differences

Sex differences play a very important role in the development of personality. Boys are generally more assertive and vigorous and prefer to have adventurous life. Girls are quieter, emotional and social as compared to boys.

(e) Nervous System

The nature of nervous system also influences the personality of an individual.

(II) Environment

The personality of an individual develops in a social environment. In this environment he develops moral ideas, social attitudes and interests. This leads to the development of social 'self' which is another expression for personality. The important aspects of the environment are as follows:

(i) Physical Environment

It includes the effect of climatic conditions of a particular region on an individual and his living.

(ii) Social Environment

An adolescent is born in a society. He spends his life in a society. Adolescence is considered to be the most important stage as he has to learn several social responsibilities by playing the role of son, brother; student etc. throughout his life. Hence, the social environment plays an important role in the development of personality. Inter-personal relations among the members of a society also help in the development of certain social personality characteristics like attraction towards others, concept of friendship, love, sympathy, hostility etc.

(iii) **Family Environment**

Home is the first learning environment for a child where he comes in contact with his parents and other family members. During adolescence period he develops his likes, dislikes, stereotypes about other people. He also has a fear of insecurity. Economic conditions of the family also affect his behavior. All these experiences help in constituting his personality.

(iv) **Cultural Environment**

The cultural environment which includes cultural traditions, ideals and values etc. also has an impact on the development of an adolescent's personality.

(v) School Environment

As an adolescent spends a significant part of his life in school so the environment of school also help in molding his personality. The school poses new problems for them, new taboos to be accepted into the superego and new models for identification, all of which contribute in molding personality. Language which he learns at school and home is an important means of communication for him as he has to interact with other members in his society, so language plays an important role in developing his personality.

(Ill) Psychological Factors

These include our motives, acquired interests, our attitudes, our will and character, our intellectual capacities such as intelligence i.e., the abilities to perceive, to observe, to imagine, to think and to reason. Self concept also influences the personality development of adolescents. Highly positive or negative thoughts help in developing the personality of an individual. These factors decide how we react in various situations and thus affect our personality.

Personality Traits

The trait theory of personality is one of the most commonly accepted theories. Several taxonomies of personality have been proposed; one of the most popular is Costa and McCrae's (1992) Five-Factor Model (FFM), which includes Neuroticism, Extraversion, Openness, Conscientiousness and Agreeableness-- known collectively as the 'Big Five'.

1. Neuroticism

Highly neurotic individuals display a lot of anxiety and hostility towards others. They feel apprehensive, nervous and worried about themselves and others. They lack sympathy for others. While individuals low in neuroticism is less anxious and easygoing. Neurotic individuals always feel sad and feel hopeless in their outlook on life. Their self consciousness hung up on how others perceive them. They show impulsiveness ie they are spontaneous in decision making. They are also vulnerable in nature. Even though this trait often has negative connotations, some of the facets are important for all individuals in moderate amounts, such as being vulnerable, impulsive and self conscious.

2. Extraversion

Introverts focus more on their own inner world while extraverts exert their energy externally in the world around them. Individuals high on extraversion tend to be more outgoing and enjoy the company of others. They also have a more positive view of the world. They are kind, friendly and risk takers. They are assertive and active with lots of interest and hobbies. They are enthusiastic and see the bright side of the things.

3. Openness to Experience

This trait involves the tendency to fantasize, be aware of one's emotions, a preference for novelty, sensitivity to art and beauty, intellectual curiosity and a tendency to be liberal in values. Openness implies a willingness to adopt innovative and unconventional ways of thinking and behaving. Individuals who are high in openness display flexible behavior. They have moral standards and principles by which they lead their life.

4. Agreeableness

Individuals high on this trait are easy going, trusting and benevolent to others. They are straightforward and frank in dealing with others. They are selfless and have great concern for others. Whereas individuals who score low have rigid thinking and behavior; they find difficulty in changing their routines.

5. Conscientiousness

This trait refers to an individual's desire to achieve and succeed. Individuals high in this trait are competent and orderly, and determined to assert their best effort. They aim to adhere to high standards of conduct. They are cautious and thoughtful in making and caring out plans. Conscientiousness most consistently predicts both academic performances as well as discipline choice. In other words, this trait not only predicts how well the individual does in a subject, but their choice of subject as well. Conscientiousness is also positively correlated with job performance and success.

Personality Development

Personality development occurs by the continuing interaction of temperament, character, and environment. Personality is what makes a person a unique person, and it is identifiable soon after birth. An adolescents' personality includes temperament, environment, and character. Temperament is the set of traits that determine how the child learns about the world. A second component of personality is related to child's specific environment which affects the individual's personality. Temperament, with its dependence on genetic factors, is referred to as "nature," while the environmental factors are called "nurture." The third component of personality is character which includes emotional, cognitive, and behavioral patterns. It also determines how a person thinks, feels, and behaves. An individual's character continues to evolve throughout life.

High-quality parenting plays a critical role in the development of a child's personality. When parents understand how their child reacts to certain situations, they can prepare him for the situation or train them to avoid a potentially difficult situation. Parents who adapt best parenting style to the particular temperament of their child can ensure successful development of their child's personality.

Adolescence is a time for change as the young person faces many new experiences. Depending on the cultural contexts, the various environments in which the adolescent moves are likely to present new and unexpected situations that require responses that the adolescent may have never previously used. Dealing with the unexpected and being required to use new untested responses is likely to raise anxiety and cause stress in the young person. The period of adolescence is the most critical period of individual's life. In this period equilibrium of physical, mental and social forces is lost, and the result is that the individual has to make new adjustments with his own self, with the family and with the society at large. Therefore adjustment to various situations is considered to be a challenge for adolescents they are supposed to deal with.

Adjustment

The term adjustment refers to a degree to which an individual's personality functions efficiently in the world of people. It refers to the harmonious relationship between the person and the environment. A well adjusted personality can efficiently and effectively play the roles which are expected to him within given environment. His needs are satisfied according to social needs. Adjustment means the response to the demands and pressures of social environment forced upon the individual. The demand to which individual has to react may be external or internal.

According to **Gates and others (1970)** "The term adjustment has two meanings. In one sense it is a continuous process by which a person varies his behavior to produce a more harmonious relationship between himself and environment. In other sense adjustment is a state i.e. the condition of harmony arrived at by the person whom we call adjusted".

Shaffer, L. F. (1956) defined "Adjustment as the fact or establishing a satisfactory psychological relationship between individuals and environment".

According to **McKinney, F. (1949), "**Adjustment is in essence the building of attitudes or the changing of the environment so as to meet the thwarted or unsatisfied motives".

Traxler, A. B. (1966) defines adjustment as "The most desirable state of adjustment is one in which the individual is perfectly happy and satisfied with all aspects of life".

According to **Symond, P. N. (1946)** "Adjustment can be defined as satisfactory relationship of an organism to its environment".

Skinner (1952) defined "Adjustment involves the organization of personality. This organization leads to the stability that is an active adjustment of an individual to his social and physical environment".

According to **Smith, P. A. (1961)** "A good adjustment is one which is both realistic and satisfying. At least in the long run, it reduces to the minimum the frustrations, the tension, and anxieties which a person must endure. It provides an evenness of satisfaction of the one intense drive at the expense of others".

Adjustment can be interpreted in the following ways:

(i) Adjustment as an achievement

Adjustment as an achievement means how efficiently an individual performs his duties in different situations. Business, military education and other social activities need efficient and well adjusted individuals for the progress and well being of the nation.

(ii) Adjustment as a process

It is very important for psychologists, teachers and parents. At the time of birth an individual is completely dependent on others for the satisfaction his needs but gradually he learns to control his needs. His adjustment depends on how he interacts with external environment. At the time of birth the world seems to be a big confusion for him but as he grows up he learns to make distinction among the various objects of his environment by the process of sensation, perception and conception.

Concept of adjustment

Adjustment is a kind of relationship between an individual and his environment. It is necessary for every individual to maintain his social relations. The parents try to train their children in such a way that his maximum needs are fulfilled. So, an individual should play his role properly in order to get maximum satisfaction. If he does not play his role accordingly his needs may not be fulfilled and he may get frustrated.

Types of adjustment

(i) Normal adjustment:

Normal adjustment is a kind of adjustment wherein the relationship between an individual and his environment is according to norms. A child who obeys his parents, studies regularly and behaves in a proper manner is considered to be well adjusted.

(ii) Abnormal adjustment:

If any individual shows maladjustment in a particular behavior, he shows abnormal adjustment. When the relationship between an individual is not according to norms, maladjustment occurs.

Problems of adjustment

(i) **Adjustment to physical growth:** Due to rapid growth in height, weight and physique, an adolescent sometimes feel embarrassed. He feels that he is looking odd in the company of his class fellows. The disturbing physical factors for girls are fatness, thinness, facial features, physical appearance and scars on face etc. The disturbing physical factors for boys are lack of muscular strength, fatness, unusual facial features, scars, bowed legs, lack of shoulder breadth etc. To provide adequate physical growth the adolescents should be given sufficient nourishing diet. An adolescent has excess of physical energy which should be utilized in sports, scouting social service and other hobbies.

(ii) **Adjustment to mental competition:** Because of mental development an adolescent become decisive and fault finder. He wants to broaden his mental perspective by knowing everything he comes across. Those adolescents who are mentally superior faces the problem of adjustment due to too strenuous competition to which they are subjected to by their parents and teachers. The mentally slow adolescents face the problem of adjustment as it is difficult for them to master the academic subjects. For adequate mental development of the adolescents, curriculum should be as broad as possible. Co curricular habits should be organized and reading habit should be developed in them.

(iii) **Adjustment to emotional disturbances:** Emotional disturbances in the adolescent are due to the rapidly changing physical structures, abnormal functioning of the nervous and glandular systems and his widening social experiences. The adolescent has got extreme emotions. His emotional moods vary from elation to depression. One minute the adolescent is up in the clouds, and the next he is in the depths of despair. He, sometimes, thinks of committing suicide. In extreme cases the behavior of the adolescent may be expressed in the form of an open defiance to the teacher or by destroying school property etc. In dealing with the adolescent, we must respect his individuality. Proper habits and sentiments should be developed in him. Self-governments should be introduced in the educational institutions. Discussion method should be encouraged. Emotions should be properly sublimated by introducing music, art, games and other co-curricular activities.

(iv) **Problem of home adjustment:** An adolescent, sometimes, cannot adjust himself to the conditions of home. His home adjustment problems arise due to the fact that his needs increase and his parents may not be able to meet all those needs. The adolescent starts behaving as an independent individual. He begins to assert himself. The parents refuse to give him independence; and this leads to trouble. He feels as if he is being kept in bondage by his parents. The parents should not dominate the adolescent unnecessarily, and should rather treat him as friend. The child should be given sufficient opportunities of study and the right to free thinking and independent outlook.

(v) **Problem of adjustment with friends:** At adolescent stage, boys and girls need some friends in whom they can confide their secrets and discuss matter freely. Hence friendships at this age have special significance on the one hand and a problem on the other. The friendships among girls are more emotionally charged than among boys. The girls tend to be more possessive of their best friends.

(vi) **Problem of sex adjustment:** There is sharply accelerated and rapid growth of sex life. Both the primaries as well as the secondary sex characteristics appear during this period. For normal sex adjustment, which is very essential, parents and teachers should impart sex education. Scientific terms should be used while giving relevant information.

(vii) **Problem of adjustment with society:** Some times, adolescents have to face the problem of adjustment with society. The adolescent cannot stand against the customs and traditions of the society. The demands of the society are too challenging for him to carry out. The adolescent should be dealt by the society in a sympathetic way. The importance of social values should be explained, social responsibilities should be assigned, individualities should be respected, and healthy activities for self-expression should be provided. Social security to the adolescent should be assured.

The behavior of an individual also lies in motivation. Motivation energizes an individual to behave in a particular way at a particular time for attaining some specific goal or purpose. The motivation in academic line promotes achievement motivation, which is responsible for good academic achievement. Also as in India the adolescence period is mostly spent in High school or Secondary school for the school going adolescents, a right career choice is very important to help them settle well in their future. Hence for planning their future this period is very important. A wrong career choice and lack of proper planning may also lead to unemployment.

Achievement Motivation

Motivation is an internal drive which accelerates our behavior. Some learners learn the same subject matter or task more effectively than others, some find it more rewarding and interesting than others; and some enjoy it more than others. At any given time, learners vary in the extent to which they are willing to direct their energies to the attainment of goals, due to difference in motivation.

It is a term used to explain initiating, direction, maintenance and termination of activities undertaken by living organisms. It impels or pushes our organism into activity, giving it a direction. The fluctuation or change in preference for activity or choice of goal leads to choosing one activity over the other. In general, people approach certain goals or engage in certain activities that are expected to have desirable outcomes and avoid certain activities that lead to unpleasant or aversive outcomes. However, many people do like challenges, undertake difficult tasks and seek pleasure in engaging in adventures. These persons have different kinds and levels of motivation.

Achievement motivation refers to the desire of a person to meet certain standards of excellence. It is not biological but shows a tremendous effect on human behavior. People differ in the degree to which they experience this need. Many studies conducted by researchers on achievement motivation are correlated with high scholastic performance and success in business. Such motivated people opt for moderately difficult tasks. They are future-oriented and persist more on the task.

It is acquired by children during the formative stages of social development. They learn it from their parents and socio-cultural environment. They acquire the values that they should attain a good position, social standing and distinguished status in the society.

Gasinde (2000) defined that "the urge to achieve varies from one person to the other, the urge is very high in some individuals and very low in others".

Tella (2007) has defined Achievement motivation "as a self determination to succeed in whatever activities one engages in, be it academic work, professional work, or sporting event, among others".

According to **Atkinson and Feather (1966)** "The achievement motivation is conceived as latent deposition which is manifested in over striving only when the individual perceives performance as instrument to a sense of personal accomplishment".

McClelland, David C. et al. (1953) defined it as "The achievement motivation may be associated with a variety of goals, but in general behavior adapted will involve activity with which is directed towards the attainment of some standards of excellence".

According to Good (1959), Academic achievement is defined as "the knowledge attained or skills developed in the school subjects, usually determined by test score or by mark assigned by teachers or both".

Crow, L. D. and Crow (1969), defined "Academic achievement as the extent to which a learner is profiting from instructions in a given area of learning i.e., achievement is reflected by the extent to which skill or knowledge has been imparted to him". Academic Achievement is the level of accomplishment attained in curricular subjects as a result of learning process and is measured in terms of the marks obtained at the examination.

Dunn and Dunn (1978) found it as "We first became involved with the phenomenon help slow learners narrow the gap between their ability to read and the grade level expectations help for them".

According to **Singh, A. and Singh, A. K. (2007)**, "Academic achievement is related to the acquisition of principles and generalizations and the ability to perform objectives, efficiently certain manipulations, symbols and ideas."

Achievement motive is defined in terms of the way an individual orients himself towards objects or conditions that he does not possess. If he values those objects and conditions, he may be regarded as having an achievement motive. It is an expectation to find satisfaction in difficult and challenging performances. In the field of education, it means the pursuit of excellence.

Achievement motive comes into picture when an individual knows that his performance will be evaluated, that the consequence of his actions will be either a success or a failure and that good performance will give a sense of pride in accomplishment. Hence, achievement motive may be considered as a disposition to approach success or a capacity for taking pride in accomplishment when success at one or another activity is achieved.

Today's modern society expects the adolescents to be a high achiever. The key criteria to judge one's true potentialities and capabilities are perhaps academic achievement. Academic achievement is considered to be an indicator of a child's future. Therefore, there is a great pressure on the minds of children and their parents. Research studies have proved that a supportive nurturing environment in home and school could enhance child's academic achievement. Family is the first and most important agency of socialization. It is observed that most of children who are successful and well adjusted come from families where wholesome relationships exist between children and their parents.

Achievement is a general term for the successful attainment of some goals requiring a certain effort. It is the degree of level of success in some specified area. It is the knowledge acquired and skills developed in school subjects generally indicated by marks obtained in test and examinations.

Individuals can set personal goals. A student may set a goal of high mark in an exam which proves beneficial in all areas of personal life. If one knows exactly what he wants to achieve, makes clear what to focus and improve on. Goal setting and arrangement promotes long-term vision and motivation. It focuses objectives, aspirations, acquirement of knowledge, and helps to manage resources. The higher the combination of intelligence and the motivation, the higher is the achievement. Therefore, the act of achieving or successful performing of a person regarding his higher values and objectives through scientific assessment with public acceptance is called achievement. In any type of sustainable development, there must be three sets of objectives – knowledge, skill and values. Achievement is possible for those who are concentrating on their objectives with total commitment and hard work. Indeed adolescents' achievement is due to much more than their intellectual ability.

Academic achievement is one part of the wider term Educational Growth. Thus academic achievement is defined as a measure of knowledge, understanding of skill in a specific subject or group of subjects. It refers to achievement in a separate subject or a total score of several subjects combined. It is concerned with quality and quantity of learning attained in a subject or a group of subjects after a period of instructions.

The world is becoming more and more competitive. The quality of performance has become the key factor for personal progress. Schools are taking a lot of efforts for helping students to achieve better in their scholastic endeavors.

Achievement in itself has become a power symbol and way of life. Academic achievement is the outcome of training imparted to a student by the teacher in school situation. Hence every individual is obsessed by social and psychological pressures later leads to various tensions and strains. Such resulting tensions are more often troublesome and results in performance decrements. In the area of educational measurement, the most significant achievement is certainly academic success. Thus academic achievement refers to the degree or level of success and that of proficiency attained in some specific area concerning scholastic and academic work.

Academic achievement of an individual is so far considered to be influenced in part by his ability to make adjustment to his environment, in part by his special abilities, aptitude and intelligence, which are essential part of his personality and in part by the intensity of motives which serves as the impelling factors for his activities. Academic achievement constitutes a socially enviable, equally pertinent and integral aspect of all students' lives such that all students are motivated to seek academic excellence.

Academic achievement has a great importance in personal life. There is an explosion of knowledge in all walks of life. Because of explosions of aspirations, every parent sets their goals high to educate their children. Thus academic achievement has become a case of educational growth. Good academic achievement help to develop self esteem, self respect and self confidence and it helps the individual to create a position in the competition ridden society. Success in academic subjects act as an emotional tonic and any damage done to a child in the home or neighborhood may be partially repaired by success in school or college. Importance of academic achievement can be judged when we realize fuller and happier life, which we wish for every student, would be impossible unless he has attained high degree of proficiency in his subjects. Academic achievement to a great extent predicts the future of student. At the time of admission, for entrance in job or for further studies, good academic achievement record is the only recommendation. Therefore, academic achievement is the unique responsibility of all educational institutions established by society to promote a whole sum scholastic development of the student.

Parents wish that their children should climb the steps of performance to as high a level as possible. This desire for achieving success puts a lot of pressure on students, teachers, schools, and, in general, the educational system itself. In fact, it seems as if the whole education system revolves round the academic achievement of students, though development of children in other areas is also expected from the system. Thus a lot of time and effort of the schools are used for helping students to achieve better in their scholastic performance.

Academic Achievement depends upon numerous factors which are responsible for high, average or low academic achievement of students. These factors are

1. Cognitive factor: it includes intelligence; creativity and language ability.
2. Non-cognitive factors: It includes variables such as self concept, adjustment and level of aspiration, needs motivation, aptitude, anxiety values and self-confidence.
3. Home environmental factors: It includes demographic variables i.e. socioeconomic status, residential background, parental aspiration and expectations, parental education and occupation, sex etc.
4. Social environmental factors: It includes personality, attitude, method of teaching, curriculum, emotional climate of school etc.
5. Lack of inspiration
6. Lack of faculties
7. Lack of financial support
8. Lack of infrastructural facilities
9. Lack of guidance and counseling

10. Lack of material support

11. Lack of encouragement and

12. Political influence

These factors differ from subject to subject, learners to learners, levels to levels, etc. Thus achievement means all those behavioral changes which take place in an individual as a result of learning experience of various kinds. Though our examination system lacks objectivity and a scientific picture of the real achievement yet it is the only method to get academic achievement. The examination marks obtained by students is the only record of academic achievements. In other words, the scores obtained on achievement test are the index of one's mental ability. Therefore, these scores form basis for the award of degrees, prizes or scholarship. These scores are utilized by the schools, colleges and universities for deciding the policies regarding the failure and promotions to the next higher class. Achievement scores are indicator of one's success. These scores are helpful to predict use of vocational maturity and vocational satisfaction. Achievement scores form the part of research for the construction of ability tests. Sound achievement in academic side can be well matched with the pillars on which the entire structure of personality stands.

Adolescence is a time during which the child urges for independence and strives to establish a sense of emotional autonomy. Many biological, cognitive and emotional changes take place during this period. Adolescents feel happiest when their parents can be both encouraging and accepting of the child's needs for more psychological independence.

Emotional Intelligence

Emotional intelligence means the capability of a person to manage and control his emotions and the emotions of others as well. It is the ability to identify and manage emotions of self and the emotions of others. It includes 3 skills:

1. Emotional awareness, including the ability to identify our own emotions and those of others;

2. The ability to control emotions and apply them to thinking and problem solving;

3. The ability to manage emotions, including the ability to regulate our own emotions, and the ability to cheer up or calm down other person.

Emotional intelligence is typically focused on recognition and regulation of emotions in one's self and social situations. It includes four categories: self-awareness, self-management, social awareness and relationship management.

According to **Salvoes and Mayer (1990)**, emotional intelligence includes an "ability to monitor one's own and others' feelings and emotions, to discriminate among them and to use this information to guide one's thinking and actions".

Salovey, Brackett and Mayer (2007) state that "emotional intelligence (EI) refers to the processes involved in the recognition, use, understanding and management of one"s own and other emotional states to solve emotion-laden problems and to regulate behavior.

Daniel Goleman developed a framework of five elements to define emotional intelligence:

1. **Self awareness**:

People with high EI are aware of their emotions and they don't let their feelings regulate them. They know their strengths and weaknesses, and they work on these areas so they can achieve better.

2. **Self regulation:**

This is the capability to control emotions. People who have the quality of self regulation don't become too angry or jealous, and they don't make careless decisions. They think twice or thrice before taking any action.

3. **Motivation**:

People with a high EI are keen to defer immediate results for long-term success. They are highly productive, like to have challenges, and are effective in whatever they do.

4. **Empathy**

This is the ability to identify with and understand the wants, needs, and viewpoints of those around us. Empathetic people avoid judging too quickly, and they live their lives in an open, honest way.

5. **Social skills**

People with strong social skills rather than focusing on their own success, help others to develop and shine. They are good in managing disputes, are skilled communicators, and are excellent at building and maintaining relationships.

There is no specifically defined boundary line which can distinguish between the end of childhood and beginning of adolescence, rather this phase is considered as a transitional period from childhood into adolescence. This period encompasses a set of transitions which touches upon many aspects of individuals' behavior such as personality, adjustment, academic achievement and emotional intelligence. Such study will definitely provoke the brain of future researchers. It will also help to evaluate the number of siblings in a family.

CHAPTER -2
REVIEW OF LITERATURE

Review of related literature is an important aspect of research. A review of literature gives the investigator an excellent idea of the work previously done in the field of study and helps in keeping in touch with the recent development in the field.

It involves synthetic and synoptic understanding of the research works already conducted in the same field over a period of time. It provides some insight regarding strong points and limitations of the previous studies and enables the researcher to improve his own investigation **(Panigrahi, 1999)**. It is clearly evident that review of related literature serves as a guide post not only with regard to the quantum of work done in the field but also enables one to perceive the gaps in the concerned field of research.

Thus, review of literature is a crucial element of all research with a purpose to offer an overview of significant literature published on the topic. It provides the background and justification for the research undertaken. It helps the investigator to identify gaps in the literature about the subject under consideration. It is designed to increase the area of knowledge on the subject and to provide intellectual context for the research.

There is no single boundary line that denotes the end of the childhood or beginning of adolescence, rather it is thought of as a passage from childhood into adolescence which is composed of a set of transitions and which touches upon many aspects of individuals' behavior such as personality, adjustment, achievement motivation, academic achievement and emotional intelligence. Such study will definitely provoke the brain of future researchers. It will also help to evaluate the number of siblings in a family.

The present review of literature will consider the conceptual phenomenon as well as the variables under study to assess empirical implication. Any research needs support, verification and clarification by having through critical evaluation of the literature available to the researcher to investigate the prescribed objectives of the study. The present chapter will focus on review of literature related to personality, adjustment, achievement motivation & academic achievement and emotional intelligence of single and sibling adolescents belonging to low, middle and high socioeconomic status.

PERSONALITY

Patel, et al. (2018) assessed the Personality Profile of Adolescents across gender; the two schools namely, Janta Inter Collage Fatehpur Badagavn Jalalpur Ambedkar Nager, and Kisan Inter Collage Bhasma Ambedkar Nager were selected from Ambedkar Nager District. For the collection of information, 60 students were selected randomly from that school. Those 60 adolescents student were divided into two categories in which 30 boys and 30 girls. Introversion Extroversion Inventory test (1971) developed by Dr. P.F. Aziz and Dr. (Mrs.) Rekha Gupa was used in this study. The results concluded that most of the (60%) respondents in boys sample had extrovert and (30%) respondents had introvert and only (10%) respondents had ambient. On the other hand, in girls, sample majority of the (56.66%) of respondents had extrovert and (33.33%) respondents had introvert and only (10%) respondents had ambivert. Thus it was found that (58.33%) percent respondents had extrovert.

Badi, et al. (2017) tried to explore the effect of being single or having a sibling on the personality of children. Following the OCEAN model of personality, NEO-FFI was administered on 200 students. 50 girls and 50 boys without a sibling and 50 girls and 50 boys with one sibling were selected from senior colleges in Pune city. By using 't' test the mean differences were statistically computed. Results showed that there were no significant differences between only children and children with a sibling on all five factors of personality (Openness, Conscientiousness, Extraversion, Agreeableness, and Neuroticism).

Gupta (2017) explored the personality trait of different birth orders. Sample of the study consisted of 60 college students of different birth order (20 first born, middle born, last born). Their age ranged between 17- 26 years. Selected subjects were tested by questionnaire method their psychological dimensions of neuroticism, extraversion, openness, agreeableness, and conscientiousness to assess personality traits NEO-FFI questionnaire was used. Collected data was analyzed by using ANOVA. Findings revealed that there was significant difference between different birth orders on personality traits.

Stephen, et al. (2017) investigated the relationship between sibling birth spacing and, extroversion and introversion characteristics of adolescents in Nairobi, Kenya. The study adopted mixed methods research paradigm with the correlation design. Purposive and simple random sampling techniques were used to select three schools for the study sample and participants. Twenty five students were selected from each school to make a total sample of 75 participants. The data collection instruments for the study were standardized questionnaires and observation guides. Data was collected and analyzed using Pearson correlation analysis and Analysis of Variance. The study concluded that close sibling spacing produce extraverted and highly aggressive children while extensive sibling spacing produces introverted and less aggressive children. The study further found that the only children were found to be highest in introversion and, lowest in aggressiveness and extraversion.

Salmon (2016) showed the relationships between birth order, personality and behavior. There were a number of birth order patterns in big five personality traits as well as behavioral aspects. Methodological issues sometimes led to inconsistent results, but overall, the evidence suggested that birth order indeed had a significant impact.

Shah & Jadav (2016) examined the different factors in which an individual's personality could be affected by the sequence of their birth in the family. The conclusion was that despite the widely accepted pre- conceived characteristics that is given to children based on their birth order; this debate will never entirely come to rest. Also, there was found no biological or genetic proof, which gave these studies a scientific backing. However, the assumed roles and personalities of children in a family according to their birth order are not entirely baseless and must hold some truth due to the overwhelming number of researches carried out, investigating this topic.

Damian & Bent (2015) tested birth order associations with personality traits and intelligence using Project Talent, a representative sample (N = 377,000) of U.S. high school students. Using a between-family design and several background factors (i.e., age, sex, sibship size, parental socio-economic status, and family structure), they were able to control for potential confounds, and estimate the links between birth order and outcomes across several diverse social categories. In addition to differences between firstborns and laterborns across the entire sample, they also tested birth rank trends in a sub-sample of targets from sibships of three, raised by two parents. The average absolute association between birth order and personality traits was found to be .02, whereas between birth order and intelligence was .04.

Rohrer, et al. (2015) examined the long-standing question of whether a person's position among siblings has a lasting impact on that person's life course. The research on the relation between birth order and intelligence predicted that performance on psychometric intelligence tests turn down slightly from firstborns to later-borns. They used data from three national panels from the United States to resolve this research question. This database identified even very small effects of birth order on personality. They compared siblings with different birth-order positions (i) within the same family and (ii) between different families. In their analyses, they confirmed the expected birth-order effect on intelligence. They also observed a significant decline of a 10th of a SD in self-reported intellect with increasing birth-order position, and this effect persisted after controlling for objectively measured intelligence. Most important, however, they consistently found no birth-order effects on extraversion, emotional stability, agreeableness, conscientiousness, or imagination. They concluded that birth order did not have a lasting effect on broad personality traits.

Soto Christopher, et al. (2015) found that like adults, children and adolescents could be described in terms of personality traits: characteristic patterns of thinking, feeling, and behaving. They reviewed research examining how youths' behavioral tendencies stick together into broader traits, how these traits are developed across childhood and adolescence. They concluded that there are both similarities and differences between youth and adult personality traits. They also said that full understanding of youth personality traits requires research at the connection of personality, developmental, and clinical psychology.

Kelley, et al. (2014) assumed about the effects of birth order on personality abound in popular culture and self-help books. Indeed, when one sibling was asked to compare themselves to others in their family, birth order showed weak-to-moderate effects on personality. They collected Big Five personality data on 69 young adult firstborn–laterborn sibling pairs. They also obtained data from parents of the sibling pairs and peer ratings of original participants' personality traits. Their findings were consistent with results from between-family designs and they provided further evidence, employing a within-family design that utilizes data from multiple family members, that birth order did not have enduring effects on personality.

Rechek, et al. (2014) assumed about the effects of birth order on personality abound in popular culture and self-help books. When one sibling was compared to others in their family, birth order showed weak-to-moderate effects on personality. They collected

Big Five personality data on 69 young adult firstborn–laterborn sibling pairs. They also obtained data from parents of the sibling pairs and peer ratings of original participants' personality traits. Their findings also revealed that birth order did not have enduring effects on personality.

Kochargaonkar & Balajiwala (2013) explored the relation between personality dimensions and identity crisis of adolescents if any. They observed that personality of the adolescents did not play any considerable role in causing identity crisis among adolescents. They also found that adolescents are able to cope well with their situations and people around them and live rather comfortably. The study conducted indicated that personality dimensions did not become causal factors for identity crisis.

Dhody (2012) investigated the adjustment problems of high and low SES adolescent girls with focus on their personality trait of introversion and extroversion. Sample of 100 girls' students was taken with 50 girls of high SES and 50 girls of low SES from colleges of Delhi .The tool used was Introversion Extroversion Inventory by P.F Aziz and Dr. Rekha Agnihotri .Descriptive survey method of study was followed. Scoring of the tool was done to find out the extrovert introvert and ambivert students. The study showed that there is no significant difference in introversion extroversion behavior of girls of high and low SES.

Klimstra (2012) stated that personality development is not only about changes in traits but also about changes in other layers of the self, such as the identity layer. Forming one's individuality is the key developmental task of adolescence. Profound changes in personality traits occur in this period. In this article, he summarized research on these processes, including research on adolescent personality trait development from a variable-centered and a typological point of view. He also described contemporary models to measure identity formation and addressed the importance of examining identity formation.

Savita & Duhan (2012) investigated personalities of rural and urban adolescents from disorganized families. Results indicated that rural adolescents were considerably higher in their boldness, leadership and sensitivity.

Marini & John (2011) tested in a sample of 231 college students with the NEO Five-Factor Inventory regarding birth order differences in five-factor model personality traits. Students were selected from families with two or three biological siblings. They did not select half-siblings, step-siblings, or adopted siblings. Firstborn (n = 103) and laterborn (n = 128) students were compared using NEO-FFI ratings by the self, by a same-sex college peer, and by a biological parent. No birth order differences were found between them.

Mehta (2010) studied "Personality needs and Academic Achievement of Sr. Secondary students". A sample of 120 students of X class was selected from 5 schools in Ghaziabad city. She used Meenakshi Personality Inventory. She found that need-achievement, need dominance, need nurturance and need-endurance are positively and significantly related to students' academic achievement. It was found that some students had low achievement and the cause is the low level of related need.

Swain, et al. (2010) studied sociometric status, personality characteristic and intelligence of High school students. The sample of 124 male students divided into three groups of 45, 42 and 37 was selected by using purposive sampling technique from one district of Orissa. The findings were(1) There exist a significant positive relationship between sociometric status derived from the sociometric criterion and personality factors A, E, F and Q (2) In case of 14 personality factors measured by High-School Personality Questionnaire, factors B,D,E,G,H,O and Q2 are simple measures. The remaining personality factors had emerged to be complex measures. (3) Positive personality traits had been found to be more important than negative ones in making a person popular.

Dixon, et al. (2008) showed the influence of birth order on the personality traits of siblings belonging to large families. Extraversion and Neuroticism were quantified for each participant who completed the Eysenck Personality Questionnaire. Overall, the youngest and three youngest siblings significantly differed from the oldest and oldest three siblings for Extraversion within and across families. The effects of age, gender and family size on these personality traits were examined based. An age effect was identified for Extraversion, whereas gender and family size did not have an impact.

South, et al. (2008) found significant moderation of both positive and negative qualities of the parent-adolescent relationship, such that the genetic and environmental variance in relationship quality varied as functions of the adolescent's levels of personality. These findings supported the importance of adolescent personality in the development of the quality of the parent-adolescent relationship.

Susan, et al. (2006) examined Big Five personality development across adolescence and middle adulthood. Two adolescents and their parents from 285 Dutch families rated the personality. For boys, Extraversion and Openness decreased and for girls, Extraversion, Agreeableness, Conscientiousness, and Openness increased. Whereas Emotional Stability and Conscientiousness of mothers increased, Extraversion, Agreeableness, and Emotional Stability of fathers decreased. Results confirmed that personality change is possible during life course but these changes are not similar for all individuals.

Scholte, et al. (2005) studied personality types, subtypes and psychosocial Adjustment of adolescents. A sample of 3,284 Dutch adolescent boys and girls was studied. They found that the personality subtypes were associated with very distinctive adjustment patterns.

Wang, et al. (2000) found no statistically significant differences in height, mass or BMI between the onlies and siblings. The significant difference regarding personality traits was that the onlies were found to have more somatic complaints; however, the data didn't show any other unwanted personality traits for the onlies. These results suggested that Chinese preschool children grew normally with or without sibling.

Sulloway (1997) conducted a research on birth order in siblings and concluded on the basis of that research that firstborns were more conscientious, ambitious, academically oriented, conforming, and conservative, inclined towards leadership than laterborns. They were also respectful of their parents than their later-born siblings. Children born later in the birth order tended to be more unconventional, flexible and rebellious.

Dunn and Judy (1992) studied the influence of a sibling on a growing child's personality found that children not only gain some understanding of power and conflict from these relationships but also learn vicariously about their own worth and esteem in comparison to their siblings by observing the treatment of sibling by their parents and others.

ADJUSTMENT

Bahreasemani, et al. (2015) studied to compare social adjustment, self-worthiness and achievement motivation among only- child adolescence and adolescence with sibling. In this ex post facto research, two groups of subjects (only- child adolescence =26 and adolescence with sibling =29) were selected via cluster sampling. Data collected by Adjustment Inventory Sinha and Sing (AISS), Rosenberg self-esteem scale (RSES), and Achievement Motivation Test (ACMT). They collected data analyzed using descriptive statistics (mean and standard deviation) and one-way variance analysis. The results revealed that there 0/01), there was a significant difference between both groups of adolescence in social adjustment (p 0/01). Also, results significant difference between both groups of adolecence in self- worthiness (p showed that there was a significant difference between both groups of adolescence in achievement motivation.

Bekkhus, et al. (2014) reviewed that twinning raises risk for behavioral difficulties in childhood is persistent, yet they found limited and inconsistent empirical evidence. Analyses of data from an Australian sample of twins and single-born children were taken. The outcome measured was the Strengths and Difficulties Questionnaire. They found difference between twins and single-born in mean behavioral difficulties and their relationship. Results indicated no differences in mean levels of behavioral difficulties between twins and single-born siblings.

Raina & Bhan (2014) investigated the significant differences in the Security - Insecurity scores and ordinal positions of adolescent boys and girls who belonged to nuclear and joint families. The results showed that girls showed more insecure feelings than the boys. The adolescents of nuclear families were more insecure than the adolescents from joint families. The first born adolescents were more insecure in comparison to lastborn. The middle born adolescents were more insecure than the last born.

Senguttuvan, et al. (2014) examined relations between sibling relationship qualities and adolescents' health attitudes. Results of their studies indicated that net of parent–adolescent relationship qualities and adolescents' personal characteristics, sibling intimacy was related to healthy attitudes and greater exercise behaviors, whereas sibling conflict was associated with increased risk of being overweight.

Sweeting & Hunt (2014) studied adults and adolescents, and suggested subjective socio-economic status (SES) is associated with health/well-being even after adjustment for objective SES. In adolescence, objective SES has weaker relationships with health/well-being. They investigated the associations which objective SES (residential deprivation and family affluence), subjective SES and three school-based subjective social status dimensions ("SSS-peer", "SSS-scholastic" and "SSS-sports") had with physical symptoms among 2503 Scottish 13–15 year-olds. They found inconsistent association between objective SES and health. Lower subjective SES had increased physical symptoms and psychological distress. Lower SSS-peer was associated with increased psychological distress but reduced anger. Lower SSS-scholastic was found to have increased physical symptoms, psychological distress and anger, and lower SSS-sports was associated with increased physical symptoms and psychological distress. Associations did not vary by gender. Objective and subjective SES had weaker associations with health/well-being than did school-based SSS dimensions. These findings underlined the importance of school-based SSS in adolescence, and the need for future studies to include a range of school-based SSS dimensions and several health/well-being measures. They also highlighted the need for a focus on school-based social status among those working to promote adolescent health/well-being.

Dhyani & Singh (2013) assessed and compared the adjustment level of adolescents from foster home and biological nuclear families. They found that girls from both the family settings exhibited higher level of adjustment in all the domains than boys. Besides this, majority of the respondents from both the family settings were found to be average or above in all the domains of adjustment. However approximately 25% of the population under study was seen to be having unsatisfactory adjustment level. Results also indicated that except on the educational adjustment dimension, respondents from biological nuclear families were found to be significantly more socially, emotionally and compositely adjusted than their counterparts.

Hasnain & Adlakha (2012) investigated the differences in the levels of self-esteem social maturity and well-being between adolescents with and without siblings. The results showed significant contribution of social maturity and self-esteem together in well-being of adolescents without siblings, but independently none of these factors contribute significantly to their well-being. The total contribution of self-esteem and social maturity in the well-being of adolescents without siblings was 13%. However, in the case of adolescents with siblings social maturity and self-esteem did not contribute significantly to their well-being.

McHale, et al. (2012) reviewed the literature on sibling relationships in childhood and adolescence, starting by tracing themes from foundational research and theory and then focusing on empirical research during the past 2 decades. This literature recognized siblings' importance in family life, the difference in sibling relationship qualities, and the significance of siblings for child and adolescent development and their adjustment. In big families sibling influences emerge due to intense emotional interaction between them. The results indicated that although siblings are building blocks of family structure and key players in family dynamics, their role is rather neglected by family scholars.

Deepshikha & Bhanot (2011) assessed family environment of adolescent girls and its impact on their socio-emotional adjustment. The statistical analysis showed socio emotional and educational adjustment of adolescent girls was affected by eight family environment factors such as expressiveness conflict, acceptance and caring, independence, active-recreational orientation, cohesion, organization and control.

Soli, et al. (2011) found associations between sibling relationships and adjustment among 179 African American adolescent siblings. They tested moderating effects of familism values and birth order. Their research revealed that familism values moderated sibling relationship-adjustment linkages. They also suggested that youth who reported both strong familism values and harmonious sibling relationships exhibited the most positive outcomes. These effects were more reliable for older than for younger siblings. Findings highlighted the role of cultural values and birth order in shaping sibling influence processes.

Goldstein, et al. (2010) compared parents' self-reports with self-reports from 27 children who have siblings with autism and 27 children with no disabled sibling. A qualitative analysis of data from the Child Behavioral Checklist and the quantitative analysis of the Weinberger Adjustment Inventory produced two main findings: (a) Siblings had noticeably lower levels of involvement in extracurricular activities; and (b) Parents and siblings defined the attributes 'helpfulness/responsibility' in an almost different manner. Parents considered these to be positive attributes of their healthy child, self-reports suggested that for siblings these attributes might be a source of distress.

Rainisch (2010) studied the effect of sibling relationship quality, parent-adolescent relationship quality, and perceived parental differential treatment on adolescent mental health over time. The study assessed 2,379 adolescents in the National Longitudinal Study of Adolescent Health (Add Health) in Waves 1 and 3 to consider parent-child and sibling relationship quality. This study evaluated whether perceived parental differential treatment alters sibling relationship and parent-child relationship quality effects on adolescent mental health, and whether patterns differ for adolescents in diverse family environments. Preliminary findings of ordinary least squares regression models showed that among adolescents living with only their mother, those who do not believe their mother to be warm and loving are associated with more negative mental health. The same is true for adolescents who believe their mothers do not care for them. However, these findings were not consistent for adolescents living with only their father.

Bellin (2006) tested an ecological model of adjustment for adolescent siblings using self-report surveys. The ecological model explained a significant amount of variance in sibling self-concept, pro social behavior and behavior difficulties. Significant individual risk and protective factors were observed at several layers of sibling life. There were divergent predictors of self-concept and behaviour. Birth order emerged as an important moderating variable in several regression equations.

Hindes (2006) examined mechanisms by which sibling relationships may buffer the harmful effects of negative peer experiences and the psychological adjustment of children with mental retardation (MR) or learning disabilities (LD). The study examined the effects of sibling social competency training on peer experiences and the impact of sibling relationship qualities including warmth and positivity, supportiveness, conflict and negativity on children's loneliness, internalizing and delinquent behavior problems. Results indicated that: Children with an LD or MR experienced significantly higher rates of loneliness and internalizing but not delinquent behavior problems than typically developing children.

Oliva Alfredo & Arranz Enrique (2005) analyzed sibling relationships during adolescence, within the context of parent and peer relationships, and their link with socio emotional adjustment. They found important gender-based differences in the meaning and importance that sibling adjustment seems to have for adolescents. A good relationship of girls with their siblings was linked to a good relationship with their parents and peers. They also had increased self-esteem and life satisfaction. For boys, sibling relationships had no association with other family or personal variables.

Milevsky (2005) examined how the compensatory effects of social support received from siblings relate to psychological adjustment in emerging adulthood. Participants completed measures of social support from a variety of sources and several indicators of well-being. The main conclusions were: Sibling support was associated with lower loneliness and depression and with higher self-esteem and life satisfaction. Sibling support paid for low parental and peer support. Sibling support also paid for low support from mothers for depression and self-esteem. Similarly sibling support also compensated for low support from fathers for loneliness and self-esteem. Sibling support to some extent compensated for low support from friends and completely compensated for self-esteem, depression and life satisfaction. The study revealed that potential benefits of sibling support demand a closer inspection of the wide-ranging issues concerned in sibling relations.

Ravneet (2005) studied Aggression and Adjustment among Adolescents belonging to One Child and Many Children Families in relation to Socio Economic Status and Home Environment and concluded that there was no family difference in aggression because of difference in type of family. There was no interaction effect of sex and family type on aggression. The children belonging to single child family were more socially adjusted than children belonging to multi children family. The family type and socio-economic status were found to have no effect on social adjustment of children. Children from single child family were found to have higher educational adjustment than those belonging to multi children family.

Xiaohua (2005) surveyed and found that more than 60 per cent of Chinese young people growing up without siblings said they felt lonely in their childhood. More than 58 per cent of these young people admitted they are lonely, selfish and willful. More than 66 per cent of them expressed disappointment at having no brothers or sisters with whom they can share their happiness or sorrow in life. About 46 per cent of them, who were born in the 1980s, said that they would prefer to have two children themselves.

Branjhe, et al. (2004) took a sample of 285 Dutch families with two adolescent children (11- to 15-year-olds), these two siblings judged the support perceived from each other. They themselves and their parents also examined their internalizing and externalizing problem behaviors. The results indicated that support perceived from a sibling is mostly negatively related to externalizing problems; sibling problem behavior is strongly related to internalizing problems. The results also indicated that adolescents' relationships with both older and younger siblings are characterized by modeling processes.

Hastings (2003) studied the impact upon children of having a sibling with a disability. However, those children whose siblings are suffering with autism may are at more risk than with other disabilities. In this study, data were collected on 22 siblings of children with autism. These children were rated by their mothers as having more behavior problems and fewer pro social behaviors than a normative sample. Analysis of variables predicted the behavioral adjustment of siblings and revealed that boys with siblings who have autism are engaged in fewer pro social behaviors.

Bauserman (2002) conducted a meta-analytic review on Adjustment in Joint-Custody and Sole-Custody children and the study concluded that children in joint custody were better adjusted than children in sole-custody. Joint-custody parents reported less current and past conflict than did sole custody parents but this did not explain the better adjustment of joint custody children. The results also revealed that joint custody can be advantageous for children's adjustment when both the parents are positively involved.

Gupta (2002) studied the future awareness, vocational interest and school adjustment of senior secondary students of: High Income Group and Low Income Group, Urban and Rural Background, Private and Government Schools, and High Achievers and Low Achievers. He found that the high income students have been found having more adjustment than their low income counterparts. The female students tended to have more vocational interest in the artistic and household areas and more school adjustment than the male counterparts. The urban students were found having better adjustment than rural students. The private school students tended to be high achievers and having more school adjustment than government school students. The high achievers tended to be more future aware and more adjusted with academic activity, school mates and personnel than their low achiever counterparts.

Widmer and Weiss (2000) investigated the association between older sibling support, older siblings' adjustment and younger siblings' adjustment in the areas of delinquency, academic success and mental health and found that sibling support insignificantly correlated with all three areas of developmental adjustment for younger siblings. The results of their study revealed that when children are accompanied by a positive image of their older sibling, it leads to positive developmental adjustment of younger siblings.

Conger, et al. (1997) explored the relations between Parents' and Siblings' psychological control and adolescent adjustment (i.e. self-esteem and problems of internalization and externalization).They used correlation and regression analysis to assess the association between these variables. Results of their study indicated that when parents and siblings both show psychological control the adjustment problems of adolescents increased and it also led their diminished self-confidence.

Mueller and Vandell (1995) found that children with older siblings offering an outlet for interaction were more responsive socially to other children of their own age. This interaction propels them into social situations in which they actively seek out playmates in settings away from home. The foundation for developing healthy peer relations is laid in the home at an early age. This foundation is solidified via the exposure to siblings as they communally partake in activities including social-role playing and scripts. Children are socialized as to acceptable social roles and actions within those social roles largely through interaction with their siblings.

Singh (1995) showed that the quality of relationship an adolescent has with his parents and siblings and the way an adolescent feels about the child training method used, play a vital role in deciding the sort of individual he will become. The ordinal position of the adolescent becomes more important than when he was younger because his attitude towards the role associated with this position had a greater effect on the way he feels about himself. The results indicated that during adolescence, the oldest child is expected to take responsibilities and to help with the care of younger sibling. He also suggested that taking responsibilities and looking after younger may make the oldest child feel important or martyred.

Brody, et al. (1994) developed a model to account for variation in the quality of sibling relationships across a 4-year span from middle childhood to early adolescence. They tested this model on a sample of 71 families, in which older siblings' ages ranged from 6 to 11 years, and those of younger siblings ranged from 4 to 9 years. They also assessed continuity and discontinuity over time in sibling relationship quality. The analyses of their study revealed negative sibling relationship qualities increases and positive qualities decreases over time. They also suggested that sibling relationship quality is affected by children's temperaments; inter parental conflict, positivity in parent-child relationships, and differential negativity in parent-sibling relationships.

Newman (1994) analyzed on the basis of sibling relationship that having a friendly sibling relationship with sibling is very important to have good social experiences. In order to maintain such a relationship in a positive manner requires insight into another's motives and feelings, tolerance, self control and understanding for others' behavior and incompetencies. He also suggested that spending time with sibling can help maintain a positive relationship between them.

Stocker (1994) studied links between children's psychological adjustment and individual differences in their perceptions of relationships with siblings, mothers and friends. Results indicated that these relationships were significantly correlated with children's loneliness, depressive mood and behavioral conduct. The results indicated that children whose relationships with mothers and friends were characterized by high levels of warmth had significantly better adjustment outcomes than children having low levels of warmth in relationships with both friends and mothers.

Byrd, et al. (1993) examined only children to determine whether they faced difficulty in achieving individuation and separation later in their life. The results of this experiment revealed that only children were less independent than children having siblings.

Mischel (1993) carried out his research on only children. He stated that only children usually undergo conditioning to affect their behavior in social situations. The results of this research indicated that only children have no playmates in their family so if they have to make friends, they would be conditioned to behave in an outgoing manner.

Rosenberg and Hyde (1993) predicted that all only children are not alike. Their research indicated that there may be different categories of only child females like normal, well adjusted, first born etc. Treating all these only children in the same way is not profitable for a research as they are affected many factors such as geography, age and culture. Their study suggested that parenting skills, environments and genetics play an important role in their positive upbringing.

ACHIEVEMENT MOTIVATION

Kaushal, et al. (2018) carried out a cross sectional study at Government and Private Schools of Gwalior. 1400 students were selected randomly for this research. They prepared questionnaire in Hindi and English language adapted from Educational Stress Scale for Adolescent (ESSA) and Academic Stress Scale (ASC). Their study revealed that the school going adolescents experience educational stress which is affected by age, gender, socioeconomic status, examinations, expectation from their parents and competition with peer and also found that adolescents adopted different coping strategies to deal with educational stress.

Qureshi (2017) predicted sibling spillover effects on child test score achievement using administrative school records from North Carolina. While teacher experience is a key determinant of student achievement, they assessed that teacher experience also affects the achievement of a child's younger siblings. In compare to this, teacher experience does not have an effect on the test scores of the child's older siblings. The results of the study suggested that direct sibling effects rather than parental behavior responses are more important and hence the importance of education cannot be underestimated.

Shukla (2016) attempted to study the association between number of Siblings and their academic Achievement. For this study they selected 150 students from Lovely Professional University, Phagwara through random sampling method. Data obtained regarding number of siblings and academic performance of students was analyzed by using Anova. Results depicted that there was no significant association between number of siblings and academic achievement. So from the research it was suggested that, in future variables like the role of sibling's relationship, parental education, home environment, socioeconomic status on academic achievement can be included.

Kipp (2015) explored the idea that the GPA of students is affected by having siblings at home. They also studied whether having older or younger sibling affected the academic score of a child. The study further explored the effect of gender ie whether having an older male or female sibling affected the GPA of students. The results of the study indicated that the GPA of students was not affected by having an older or younger sibling at home. The gender also didn't have any positive or negative influence on GPA. Finally it was demonstrated by results that presence of any type of siblings didn't have a significant effect on GPA.

Bartwal & Singh (2014) explored the relationship between academic stress among school going adolescents in rural and urban area. Results of their study revealed that there were no significant gender differences with regard to academic stress among rural and urban adolescents.

Chen & Liu (2014) found that for academic related outcomes there were no differences between singletons and firstborns who had any number of younger siblings. There was also no difference between singletons and laterborns from two child families. In comparison to this singletons were considered more advantageous than laterborns having two or more siblings on the grounds of educational expectations. Singletons were expected to spend more time on homework than laterborns having three or more siblings. Singletons were also not different from laterborns in terms of psychological outcomes psychological distress, peer pressure etc. Finally, the results of the study revealed that there was no significant difference between singletons and those having siblings on academic related grounds.

Franky & Chamundeswari (2014) investigated the psycho-social correlates of academic achievement of adolescent students. Analysis of data collected showed that the adjustment pattern was similar among students in boys, girls and co-education state board schools at the secondary level. It was also further seen that the co-education students were better than the boys in the socio-economic status of state board schools. It was also concluded from the study that co-education students were better than boys and girls in their academic achievement of state board schools.

Kumar, et al. (2014) studied the level of achievement motivation, psychological adjustment and emotional intelligence of school students across various Indian demographic groups. The sample comprised of 450 urban 10th grade male students from Jaipur (Rajasthan). The results of the study revealed that there was a significant difference in the social and emotional areas of psychological adjustment of students belonging to different demographic groups. They found no significant difference in their level of achievement motivation, emotional adjustment and emotional intelligence.

Ahmar & Anwar (2013) showed that gender did not influence the achievement in science at higher secondary school level. The results also showed the difference between high and low socio-economic status groups. It was found that the academic achievement was influenced by the socio-economic status and those who belonged to high socio-economic status showed better performance.

Dagys Pajoluk (2013) found that during adolescence older siblings serve as examples for younger ones. The goal of this study was to determine whether older sibling support enhances the academic achievement of younger ones. The data was collected from

288 younger siblings in ninth and tenth grades. Participants mentioned their own and their older siblings grade and complete measure of sibling intimacy. They also mentioned their family cohesion and parents expectations of achievement. The results of this study provided support that older siblings' academic engagement is a key aspect of older sibling support that relates to younger siblings' academic achievement. This study highlighted the importance of both sibling and family variables in influencing younger siblings' achievement.

Sathe & Uttam (2012) examined the relationship between Academic Achievement and Adjustment Factors among adolescent students in urban and rural areas. Results of their study showed that Academic Achievement was negatively correlated to Adjustment Factors in urban and rural adolescent students and the Adjustment Factor was positively correlated with each other.

Ha, Tshui Sun (2011) investigated birth order effect on personality and academic performance amongst 120 Malaysians. Their study also examined the relationship between personality and academic achievement. Thirty firstborns, 30 middle children, 30 lastborns, and 30 only children were selected for this study. The results of this study indicated that participants of different birth positions did not differ significantly in terms of personality and academic performance.

Ryherd (2011) tried to understand the relationship between an adolescent's older sibling and peers on their academic achievement. A sample of 217 adolescents and their older siblings were taken in this study to predict adolescent's academic achievement. The warmth and support level of positive older siblings to the peers and their academic achievement was measured in this study. The results of this study revealed that positive warmth and support from an older sibling directly influenced an adolescent's academic achievement.

Bissell-Havran (2010) associated the parents' behaviors and attitudes with adolescents' academic outcomes. This study emphasized on the interaction of only one-parent child dyad in the family. They used data from the National Longitudinal Study on Adolescent Health (Add Health) to examine whether parents' differential treatment of their offspring is associated with sibling's academic outcomes. Overall, the findings suggested that differences in academic achievement may be more strongly linked than parents' differential treatment to sisters' and brothers', but suggested the possibility that parenting factors could play a small role.

Bouchey, et al. (2010) investigated prospective relations between older siblings' support and academic engagement and younger siblings' academic adjustment from 7th to post-8th grade. The study incorporated a sample of both African American and European American adolescents. This study also investigated the extent to which the gender constellation of sibling dyads moderated prospective associations. The findings of the study revealed that younger siblings' perceptions of support established from the older sibling and their constructive image of the older sibling showed declines in the siblings' reported support to younger siblings also showed declines in younger siblings' academic adjustment. The older siblings' own level of academic engagement showed an increase in younger siblings' academic younger siblings' academic self-perceptions and performance over time. Overall, findings did not differ significantly for African and European American adolescents.

Travis & Kohli (2010) explored the relationship between birth order and academic attainment from a variety of socioeconomic backgrounds. Birth order had an impact on total years of education completed among members of the middle class families. The findings also indicated that "only" children, appear disproportionately to excel in terms of educational attainment.

Chooi (2009) determined if motivation style is the underlying construct that bridges birth order effects with intelligence, school performance and personality. Participants completed a survey to assess motivation style as measured by the tendency to activate or inhibit behavior based on learned rewarding or punishing environmental cues. The study failed to find significant birth order differences for motivational style with the exception of an inverse relationship between family size and fun seeking tendency. Larger age gap between siblings corresponds with higher reward seeking. Family size and academic achievement were negatively correlated, and the only and oldest child had higher academic achievement scores.

Kaur, et al. (2009) revealed self-concept to be positively correlated with academic achievement. This study revealed that various home environment components like protectiveness, reward and nurturance showed a significant positive relationship with self concept. It was suggested that use of rewards and nurturance from parents should be done for positive self-concept development among adolescents. However, the correlation of social isolation and deprivation of privileges was significantly negative with self-concept among adolescents. Therefore this study indicated that for positive self-concept development among adolescents, there should be no use of social isolation and deprivation of privileges.

Tavares, et al. (2004) assessed the impact of being an only-child on characteristics of parental and peer relationships, school achievement, social, and sexual behavior. A sample of three hundred and sixty adolescents at the third year of high school from a private school at Porto Alegre was selected for the study. The sample was assessed by giving a questionnaire containing information schooling of parents, birth order, alcoholic consumption, drug use and school achievement etc. Only-children were less likely to report an episode of alcohol intoxication than first-born and adolescents with siblings. They concluded that the status of being an only-child is not associated with a poorer outcome in several areas of the development.

Wan, et.al (1994) investigated the behavioral traits Chinese, urban only children as they realized that the number of only children are increasing rapidly. They developed an inventory consisting of 27 items covering three behavioral traits. These three behavioral traits were achievement motivation, interpersonal skills and attitude toward manual labor. The analysis revealed that only children exceeded the sibling children on achievement motivation. Only children did not differ significantly on interpersonal skills and attitude toward manual labor.

Falbo & Poston (1993) compared the outcomes of only children to those of firstborn and later-born children. The results of the study indicated that in terms of academics, differences between only children and others were found. Onlies scored more in verbal tests. In terms of personality, very few only-child effects were found.

EMOTIONAL INTELLIGENCE

Neanam (2018) studied the emotional intelligence of adolescent belonging to upper socioeconomic status, middle socioeconomic status and lower socioeconomic status. A group of 150 adolescents (50 from each socio economic strata) was selected from both government and private institutions via a stratified random sampling technique. The data were collected using an Emotional Intelligence Inventory and Socio Economic Status Scale

(SESS) and analyzed using mean, S.D and F-test. The findings of the study indicated that there is some difference. The higher mean value in favors of upper and middle socioeconomic status" adolescents further indicated that they had significantly higher emotional intelligence as compared to the lower socioeconomic adolescents student. But these differences didn't alter the F- ratio so it was concluded from the above analysis that variation in socio-economic status (SES) levels didn't associate with variation in emotional intelligence in adolescent students. It was further concluded that there exists no significant difference in the emotional intelligence level of upper, middle and lower socioeconomic groups of adolescent students.

Tyagi & Komal (2018) aimed to study the emotional intelligence of adolescent students in relation to their Gender and Locality. 200 senior secondary students were the sample of study and they selected through stratified random sampling method from senior secondary schools of Ghaziabad district of Uttar Pradesh. For the collection of necessary information investigator used Emotional Intelligence Inventory-MEII by Dr. S.K. Mangal and Shubra Mangal. The results of this research inferred that secondary school students those studied in schools of urban locality in Ghaziabad district of Uttar Pradesh had better EI than the students of schools of rural areas but gender wise students did not differ significantly on emotional intelligence.

Bala & Arora (2017) investigated the interpersonal skills of single adolescents and adolescents having siblings. It was based on the hypothesis that there is no significant difference between the interpersonal skills of single child adolescents and adolescents having siblings as perceived by peer group and teachers. The size of sample was 400, comprising 200 single child adolescents and another 200 adolescents having siblings of district. Sirsa, Haryana. A self constructed and standardized scale consisted 72 items for peer group and 50 items for teachers was designed by the investigator. Ex- post facto research method was used. The data was analyzed using t-test. The findings revealed no significance difference in the level of interpersonal skills of single child adolescents and adolescents having siblings.

Ghanawat, et al. (2016) assessed the relationship between family functioning and emotional intelligence among adolescents. The sample of the study included 52 adolescents studying in 11th and 12th standard. They used " Mangal Emotional Intelligence Inventory" and "Family Functioning Questionaire" to assess emotional intelligence and family functioning respectively. They found a significant positive correlation between family functioning and emotional intelligence. They also found that healthy family relationship help in developing better emotional intelligence.

Habeeb & Fatema (2016) studied the intrapersonal dimension and interpersonal dimension of emotional intelligence and its impact on stress management. Descriptive survey method was used to conduct the study and Random sampling technique was used for the selection of the sample. They used Emotional intelligence inventory and Stress Management Scale for the collection of data. The statistical measures used for the analysis and the interpretation were Pearson's co-efficient of correlation, mean, S.D and t-test. The findings revealed that intrapersonal and interpersonal awareness are positively and significantly correlated to each other. There was no significant difference found between the intrapersonal and interpersonal awareness of male and female adolescent students but significant difference was found in the stress management level of male and female adolescents of Aurangabad city.

Lekaviciene, et al. (2016) emphasized the significant role of family in the development of personality in the childhood. He found out that social and psychological family factors are essential for the development of emotional intelligence. The majority of subjects in the study were high school students. It was revealed from the study that EI level is statistically significantly related to some family factors like psychological climate in the family, strength of relations with their parents and financial status etc.

Jamadar, et al. (2015) investigated the impact of socioeconomic status on emotional intelligence and creativity among tribal students. They took 100 tribal samples who belonged to 8, 9 and 10th class. The sample comprised of 50 boys and 50 girls from Vivekananda Tribal Centre for learning (VTCL), Hosahalli, H.D.Kote, Mysore. The Socio Economic Status scale by Meenakshi(2004), Emotional Intelligence by Upinder Dhar (2010)was taken. The results of the study revealed that high socioeconomic status students have more emotional intelligence and creative than the low socioeconomic status students. There was no effect of gender found on emotional intelligence and creativity.

Kamath (2015) found that the topic of birth order is a popular research variable in the field of psychology, and emotional intelligence, although relatively new, is being vigorously studied by researchers in the field. Adler described birth order as the ordinal position one attains within the family. Emotional intelligence, on the other hand, can be reduced down to one common definition of understanding and interpreting one's own as well as others' emotions. This study aimed to explore the relationship between these two variables and the differences one may experience in levels of emotional intelligence based on birth order. Hypotheses developed assumed that mean differences will be observed in the (five) competencies of emotional intelligence based on birth order. A target population of 40 Indian students from the city of Mumbai participated in the study and nominated 3 raters each as well. However, the results of the study yielded no significant mean differences between the two variables, and all five hypotheses were negated. Additional analysis of gender partially supported the hypothesis that gender would produce mean differences in emotional intelligence.

Rauf (2015) investigated the effect of birth order and gender on the emotional intelligence of adolescents. The sample consisted of 200 students from grades 4th to 7th. The results revealed the interaction of birth order and gender on emotional intelligence but they found no significant difference among the groups.

Saikia, et al. (2015) tried to find out the emotional intelligence levels of adolescents and to find out the differences among them due to different socio cultural background. The sample size comprised of 325 adolescents (16-18 years) drawn from urban, rural and tribal areas of Jorhat district of Assam. The results revealed that the level of emotional intelligence of most of the adolescents was far better in the dimension of interpersonal management. Majority of adolescents were least competent in the abilities pertaining to the dimension of intrapersonal management. Majority of adolescents of urban culture were found to have more skills in all the dimensions of emotional intelligence than the adolescents of rural culture barring interpersonal management. The adolescents of tribal culture possessed considerably low level in all the dimensions of emotional intelligence.

Alekseeva, et al. (2014) studied associations between relationships in sibling pair and cognitive skills. The sample included 160 full families with two children of adolescent age. Family relationships diagnostic techniques and intellectual test were used. Elder children were revealed to be more inclined to conflict dominant behavior towards their siblings than younger ones. Antagonism in sibling pair was related to low levels of parents' acceptance and emotional closeness between parents and children. They concluded that children with low IQ score are more likely to dominate in sibling pair. The firstborns who demonstrate higher IQ scores are more likely to cooperate with younger sibling.

Benny (2014) studied to understand the emotional status of English medium secondary school students in Mumbai city. There were various factors that contributed and influenced the emotional competence of an individual. The dependent variable of the study was emotional quotient of adolescents while independent variables were causes of family environment like structure of family, number of family members, order of birth, parental educational qualification and occupation. The study compared all the above mentioned factors on the basis of gender as well. Stratified random sampling and purposive sampling techniques were adopted for the selection of schools while the participants were chosen based on random sampling technique. 641 boys and 610 girls of age group 13 – 16 years (N = 1251) constituted the sample. For inferential analysis of the hypotheses, t test and one way ANOVA was applied. They found, one third of the sample exhibited high level of emotional competence where as one percent participants had low EQ. Female adolescents had significantly higher emotional quotient than male adolescents. There was no significant difference in the emotional status of children irrespective of their upbringing in nuclear or joint family, with or without any siblings. The order of birth also did not notably affect the emotional quotient of adolescents.

Alkema (2013) assessed the children from two after school clubs and one church youth group. Twenty-three sibling pairs volunteered for the study. Children ranged in age between 8 and 14. Most of the children were from middle class, intact families and had low to moderate levels of conflict within the sibling relationship. It was concluded that sibling warmth and empathy are related. However, overall sibling relationship quality and emotional competence did not appear to be significantly correlated due to the lack of significant correlations found between factors within these two areas. It was also concluded that there may be differences in the way these two areas were developed. Sibling relationship quality appears to be more of an individual perception based on age and birth order whereas emotional competence appears to be a learned trait that is shared between siblings.

Sharma & Sahni (2013) revealed that level of emotional intelligence of adolescents was moderate. They found significant independent effect of home environment and personality on emotional intelligence; and significant two factor interactive effect of variables on emotional intelligence of adolescents.

Medina, et al. (2013) focused on determining the differences that exist between the Self-Reported Emotional Intelligence (SEI) of only children and first-born children and, on the other hand, the degree of perceptual adjustment of parents regarding their children. The sample was composed of 405 participants in total including only children and first-born children. The instruments used to measure emotional intelligence were the TMMS-24 (self-report emotional intelligence scale) and the PTMMS-24 (perceived emotional intelligence scale). Results showed a clear disadvantage in terms of SEI for only children compared with first-born children. They found that parents of only children have a better capacity to perceive their own child's emotions as compared with parents of first-born children.

Bhatia (2012) studies the effect of family relationship on the emotional intelligence of adolescents. The results obtained from the study revealed that healthy family relationship between parents, grandparents, siblings and other family members greatly influenced the emotional intelligence of adolescents.

Rodrigues & Abhyankar (2012) conducted a study to measure trait anger, anger expression, anger control and emotional intelligence in young adults who have no siblings and those who had at least one sibling. The sample consisted of boys and girls between the age group of 17 to 24 years (N = 160). Spielberger's State Trait Anger Expression Inventory (STAXI) was used to measure trait anger, anger expression and anger control, while Thomas and Sushama's Emotional Intelligence Inventory (EII) was used to measure emotional intelligence. Data were analyzed using independent samples t-test. No significant differences were found between young adults with siblings and those without siblings, indicating that there are no major personality differences between the two.

Mimrot (2011) studied the role of area of residence on the development of emotional intelligence and self concept of adolescents. The emotional intelligence of the subjects was measured by Emotional Intelligence Scale (EIS) of Anukool Hyde, Sanjyot Pethe and Upinder Dhar. Authors found significant differences between mean score of adolescents in urban and rural area on Emotional Intelligence. They concluded that, adolescents in urban area develop significantly better Emotional Intelligence than that of rural Adolescents.

Naghavi & Redzuan (2011) reviewed empirical studies which emphasized on the relation between gender and emotional intelligence. They told that emotional quotient (EQ) is a set of abilities such as conception, emotion appraisal and expression, emotion management and regulation and emotion utilization of emotion. Parents and children expose their emotions in an expressive way to one another, either consciously or unconsciously in their interactions. It seems that further there are individual differences between the characteristics of boys and girls. Girls are mostly expected to be more expressive of feelings than boys. The research showed that emotional intelligence is meaningfully associated with gender differences. They concluded it is important to realize that girls are higher than boys in emotional intelligence, but high emotional intelligence in boys is a better predictor for achievement.

Hafen and Brett (2010) examined the relations among the Big-five personality trait, emotional intelligence and happiness of male-female university students. Their findings revealed that specifically for females, emotional intelligence mediated association from conscientiousness and emotional instability to happiness, while males evidenced only direct association. The findings suggested different associations than those of past studies regarding personality and happiness in western sample. According to this study, results from an Indian sample, showed that emotional intelligence may serve as an intermediary from personality to happiness for females, but has independent contributions to happiness for males.

Ranjha and Shujja (2010) examined the relationship between emotional intelligence and adjustment in nurses serving in emergency and nonemergency wards of private and government hospitals. Bar-On EQ-I(1997) and Psychological Adjustment Scale (Sabir, 1999) were used to assess emotional intelligence and psychological adjustment respectively among adolescents. A demographic form was used to collect the data on other variables, specially, type of hospitals. Simple regression analysis indicated that type of hospitals (Private, government) emerged as significant predictor of emotional intelligence.

Doron (2009) examined the connection between an individual's traits, emotional functioning and role division which are influenced by birth order in the family. Sixty nine subjects were taken for the study. The subjects were first borns, middle or youngest children in their family. The subjects were administered questionnaires which measured their traits and emotions. They were also administered a role division questionnaire which measured their role division. According to study's hypothesis, a correlation was found between the emotions expressed in the sibling system and in the couple system. They found the traits to be significantly correlated between the sibling and the couple systems for first borns and middle children. In contrast to this, no effect was found of birth order, on role division in the couple system.

Kirkcaldy, et al. (2009) studied a sample of around 2,500 adolescents in a child and adolescent psychiatry clinic in the region of Münster, Germany and assessed their intelligence. Family size (total number of siblings within a family) was significantly found to be correlated with intelligence score. First borns and only children showed higher IQs than later borns. The results revealed that relationship between birth order and intelligence was moderated by gender.

Jazaeri (2008) examined the role of emotional intelligence in predicting cultural adjustment among students in Indian Students from four regions i.e. Middle East, African, East Asian, Western and European countries participated in the study. They pursued their studies in various courses at five Universities located in Mysore, Bangalore, Pune, Hyderabad and Delhi. Stepwise regression analysis revealed that positive impression, general mood, adaptability and interpersonal components of emotional intelligence were significant predictors of cultural adjustment.

Sparkman and Austin (2008) conducted a study on emotional intelligence, which is considered as a predictor of student's retention and performance overtime. Their study suggested that there is a statistically significant relationship between empathy, social responsibility, impulse control, flexibility and enrollment status and graduation status. The emotional subscales, that positively predictor were self actualization, social responsibility and happiness.

Bhandarkar (2007) conducted a study on 900 Junior college students of Nagpur district of Maharashtra. The aim of the investigation was to study the differences in Emotional Intelligence among students living in rural and urban area. Significant differences were found in Emotional Intelligence among the students. Rural students were found emotionally more intelligent than urban students.

Pastey & Aminbhavi (2006) studied to find out the impact of emotional maturity of adolescents on their stress and self-confidence. The students having high emotional maturity were compared with the students having low emotional maturity. The findings of the study revealed that adolescents with high emotional maturity exhibited high stress and self confidence than adolescents who had low emotional maturity. Adolescents with more number of siblings had shown significantly higher level of self-confidence than their counter parts. It was also found that educational level of father had significantly influenced stress of their adolescent children. Adolescent boys tend to have significantly higher stress than girls and girls tend to have significantly high self-confidence.

Ciarrochi, et al. (2001) found that EI reliably measured in adolescents, was higher for females than males, and was positively associated with skill at identifying emotional expressions, amount of social support, extent of satisfaction with social support, and mood management behavior. These relationships held even after controlling self-esteem and trait anxiety.

Morand (1999) studied and examined the link between family size and intelligence and found a consistent negative relationship. Children born into larger families tend to score lower on intelligence tests than children raised in smaller families. One recurrent but unexplained finding is that the relation between intelligence and number of siblings is consistently significant for verbal intelligence but inconsistent for nonverbal intelligence. He conceptualized emotional intelligence as one facet of nonverbal intelligence. The research developed a measure of emotional intelligence and used it to test the hypothesis that emotional intelligence is positively correlated with family size.

CHAPTER -3
METHOD AND PROCEDURE

Methodology refers to the plan, structure and strategy conceived so as to obtain answers to the research questions and to control variance. The methodology is the blue print of research investigation. It tends to include a complete outline of what the investigator did from writing of the hypotheses and their operational implication to the final analysis of the data. It enumerates the research design that is invented to enable the researcher to answer the research questions as validity, objectivity, accurately and economically as possible.

This chapter deals with the description of the sampling details, the details of the design, tests employed for gathering data, procedure for conducting the study and statistical methods to be used for analysis. The methodological details of the study are organized under the following heads:

1. Objectives of the study
2. Hypotheses
3. Variables of the study
4. Research Design
5. Locale of the study
6. Sample selection
7. Tools and Test used
8. Procedure
9. Statistical Analysis

1. Objectives:

Following objectives were set up for investigation in the present study:-

1. To study and compare the personality of single and sibling adolescents.
2. To study and compare the adjustment of single and sibling adolescents.
3. To study and compare the achievement motivation of single and sibling adolescents.
4. To study and compare the emotional intelligence of single and sibling adolescents.

5. To study the impact of socio-economic status on personality of adolescents belonging to low, moderate and high SES.
6. To study the impact of socio-economic status on adjustment of adolescents belonging to low, moderate and high SES.
7. To study the impact of socio-economic status on achievement motivation of adolescents belonging to low, moderate and high SES.
8. To study the impact of socio-economic status on emotional intelligence of adolescents belonging to low, moderate and high SES.
9. To find out the inter co-relation between various psychological variables.

2. Hypotheses:

1. There will be no significant difference between the personality of single and sibling adolescents.
2. There will be no significant difference between the adjustment of single and sibling adolescents.
3. There will be no significant difference between the achievement motivation of single and sibling adolescents.
4. There will be no significant difference between the emotional intelligence of single and sibling adolescents.
5. There will be no significant difference between the personality of adolescents belonging to low, moderate and high socioeconomic status.
6. There will be no significant difference between the adjustment of adolescents belonging to low, moderate and high socioeconomic status.
7. There will be no significant difference between the achievement motivation of adolescents belonging to low, moderate and high socioeconomic status.
8. There will be no significant difference between the emotional intelligence of adolescents belonging to low, moderate and high socioeconomic status.
9. There will be no significant inter co-relation between various psychological variables.

3. VARIABLES:

The variables included in the research investigation are as follows:

INDEPENDENT VARIABLES:

(A) TYPE OF ADOLESCENTS

(A1) Single Adolescents

(A2) Sibling Adolescents

(B) TYPE OF SOCIOECONOMIC STATUS

(B1) Low Socioeconomic Status

(B2) Moderate Socioeconomic Status

(B3) High Socioeconomic Status

DEPENDENT VARIABLES:

(1) Personality

(2) Adjustment

(3) Achievement Motivation

(4) Emotional intelligence

INCLUSION CRITERIA

Single adolescents from low socio economic status

Single adolescents from moderate socio economic status

Single adolescents from high socio economic status

Sibling adolescents from low socio economic status

Sibling adolescents from moderate socio economic status

Sibling adolescents from high socio economic status

Age of the respondents between 13- 18 years

EXCLUSION CRITERIA

Number of sibling adolescents

Male or female sibling

4. RESEARCH DESIGN

To find out the effect of independent variables on dependent variables, 2x3 factorial design was formulated. There were 6 experimental groups and 30 subjects in each group with 2 independent variables. The research design is as follows:

Table – 3.1: RESEARCH DESIGN

TYPE OF ADOLESCENTS	SOCIO ECONOMIC STATUS			Total (N)
	LOW	MODERATE	HIGH	
SINGLE	30	30	30	90
SIBLING	30	30	30	90
Total (N)	**60**	**60**	**60**	**180**

Total number of respondents in sample = 180

The six experimental groups mentioned in the above table 3.1 are as follows:

Exp.Group 1 – Single adolescents belonging to low socio economic status.

Exp.Group 2 – Single adolescents belonging to moderate socio economic status.

Exp.Group 3 – Single adolescents belonging to high socio economic status.

Exp.Group 4 - Sibling adolescents belonging to low socio economic status.

Exp.Group 5- Sibling adolescents belonging to moderate socio economic status.

Exp.Group 6- Sibling adolescents belonging to high socio economic status.

5. LOCALE OF THE STUDY:

First the area of research was selected and the problem was defined. The locale of the present study was confined to Udaipur city of Rajasthan.

6. SAMPLE SELECTION

Sampling is a process of selecting relatively small number of individuals or objects or events and analyzing them in order to find out something about the entire population from which it is selected.

A sample of 180 respondents was selected by random sampling method for the study. Out of the total sample, 30 respondents were from single adolescents belonging to low socio economic status, 30 respondents from single adolescents belonging to moderate socio economic status, 30 respondents from single adolescents belonging to high socio economic status, 30 respondents from sibling adolescents belonging to low socio economic status, 30 respondents from sibling adolescents belonging to moderate socio economic status, 30 respondents from sibling adolescents belonging to high socio economic status, The respondents belonged to the age group of 13-18 years. The criteria for selecting adolescents from different socio economic status were as follows:

Low socio economic status: Annual income < 1 lac
Moderate socio economic status: Annual income between 1 lac – 3 lacs
High socio economic status: Annual income > 3 lacs

7. DESCRIPTION OF THE TESTS AND TOOLS USED

Like other research method, collection of data, their tabulation, interpretation, logical and skillful reporting are needed. The researcher will require many data gathering tools which may vary in their complexity, design, administration, and interpretation. The researcher has to select from the available tools, which will provide data he seeks for testing the hypothesis.

In the present study standardized questionnaires have been used for data collection. Visits were made to some schools and interview of adolescents were taken in order to develop insight into different aspects like personality, adjustment, achievement motivation and emotional intelligence of single and sibling adolescents.

In the present research, following tests were used to measure different variables of the study:

TABLE: 3.2: LIST OF TESTS

S. NO.	ASPECTS STUDIED	NAME OF THE TEST	AUTHOR
1.	Personal Information Schedule	Client Information	Self Prepared
2.	Personality	Eysenck's Maudsley Personality Inventory (M.P.I.)	Eysenck, 1975
3.	Adjustment	Adjustment Inventory of School Students (AISS)	Sinha & Singh, 1971
4.	Achievement Motivation	Achievement Motive Test(ACMT)	V. P .Bhargav, 1994
5.	Emotional Intelligence	Emotional Intelligence Inventory	S.K.Mangal & Shubhra Mangal,1971

To conduct the present research study the above Test / Tools were administered on the respondents in order to collect the research data. The descriptions of the tests are as follows and tests are attached in the Appendix for references.

1. The Personal Information Schedule:

This schedule was developed to collect the following facts about the respondents:

(a) Demographic characteristics – Name, Sex, Age, Residence, Caste.

(b) Educational Information.

(c) Family background–occupation and family income.

(d) Type of adolescents (single and sibling adolescents) and birth order.

(e) Socio economic status

2. Eysenck's Maudsley Personality Inventory:

Eysenck's Maudsley Personality Inventory was constructed by Eysenck (1975). This inventory is designed for assessing Neuroticism-stability and introversion-extraversion dimensions of personality. It is suitable for normal and abnormal adults and also for adolescents. This test can be used as a group of an individual test, for persons of ages 15 to 16 years and above. Although the time limit is enforced in the testing, but the short-scale takes about 3 to 5 minutes, while the long scale takes about 15 to 20 minutes. Items from serial number 1 to 12 given on the front page of the test booklet make the short-scale. Each of these items is answerable by making a tick-mark into one of the three boxes, marked with instructions to answer the questions is given on the front cover page of the test booklet.

The 48 items of the test booklet are distributed among the two personality dimensions. Each item has three response alternatives, scored 0, 1, 2 from lower to higher levels of neuroticism and extraversion, and any single item contributes to only one of the two dimensions. The total composite neuroticism or extraversion score is simply the sum of raw scores on all the 24 items in the two dimensions. This amount to an approximately equal weighting of each dimension in its contribution to total personality stability, because the raw score means and standard deviation are approximately equal for each dimension.

This scale indicates that the differences among average scores for the sexes are insignificant, being 23.536 for M(male), and 23.232 for F(female) on N; and 26.904 and 27.796 on E respectively. The situation is similar for the short scale, being 7.14 for male, and for female on N; and 8.554 and 8.87 on E respectively. Pearson R between the L and S is 0.730 for N and +0.511 for E.

3. **Adjustment Inventory (Dr. A.K.P. Sinha and Dr. R.P. Singh):**

This is a widely used adjustment inventory in research work. It measures the adjustment of secondary school students in three areas of adjustment: Emotional, Social and Educational. The inventory has 60 items distributed equally among the three areas of adjustment. Out of those 60 items, 20 items are meant for measuring Emotional adjustment, 20 items for Social adjustment and 20 items for Educational adjustment. Scoring each item in the tool has two answers 'Yes' or 'No'. The subject is to read the statement and to see whether it applies to his mode of behavior or not. If a particular statement is true or mostly true to subject's behavior, then he is to encircle 'Yes'. On the other hand if a particular statement is false or mostly false to his behavior then he is to encircle 'No'. There is no time limit for answering it. Ordinarily an individual takes 10 to 15 minutes in completing the test. Inventory can be scored by hand only. For any answer pointing out adjustment, zero is given; otherwise a score of one is awarded. The total score on adjustment is obtained by adding up the individual scores that indicates the general adjustment status. It means high score in any given area of adjustment indicates poor adjustment and low score indicates healthy adjustment i.e. as we will move from low score to high score there will be decline in adjustment in given areas of adjustment. Scores greater than 11 on the emotional domain specify unstable emotions while low scores indicate stable emotions. Individuals with scores greater than 11, on the social adjustment domain point out that they are submissive and revering. Scores greater than 11 or above on the educational domain show that adolescents are poorly adjusted with their curricular and co-curricular programs while low scores indicative that they have interest in school programs. Reliability Coefficient of reliability was determined by (i) Split-half method (ii) Test Re-test method and (iii) K-R formula 20. The split half reliability is 0.95, the test retest reliability is 0.93 and the K-R formula reliability was found to be 0.94. Validity coefficient was determined by biserial correlation method significant level being .001. Inter-correlation among the three areas of the inventory was calculated.

4. Achievement Motivation (V. P. Bhargava)

The present test is intended to measure the N Ach score of the person. The test consists of 50 items of incomplete sentences/item which are to be completed by the subjects by putting a check-mark on any one of the three alternative responses given against each item. It is expected that the subject while engaged in the process of checking the item would consider all the possible aspects which may be thought of about the item at that time. Thus, his check on the alternative responses would indicate his true feelings. In this way all the items are to be checked indicating his responses on the whole test. The usual time which is needed for administering the test is 30 minutes including the time needed for giving the instructions to the subjects. It is desirable that the administrator while giving the test to the subjects should get them seated in such a way that they may not talk to each other or consult each other. The scoring can be done with the help of a scoring key. Each item indicating Achievement Motivation (N -Ach) is given a score of one and the total score earned on all the items is the N-Ach score. The test retest reliability for Hindi test after an interval of one month was 0.87. For English version the values of validity indices were 0.85.

5. Emotional intelligence (Dr S. K. Mangal & Shubhra Mangal)

Emotional Intelligence Inventory has been designed for the measurement of emotional intelligence of school or college going students in respect of four areas of emotional intelligence. These four areas include the following:

(a) Intra-personal awareness (Knowing about one's own emotions),

(b) Inter-personal awareness (Knowing about others emotions),

(c) Intra-personal management (Managing one's own emotions) and

(d) Inter-personal management (Managing others emotions).

It has 100 items, 25 each from the four areas to be answered as yes or no. Scoring can be done by hand or with the help of stencil. The mode of response is either yes or no indicating complete agreement or disagreement with the proposed statement respectively. 'Yes' indicates the presence of emotional intelligence and 'No' for the absence of emotional intelligence. One mark is provided for the response indicating presence of emotional intelligence and zero for the absence of emotional intelligence. Split half method (0.89), K-R formula (0.90) and Test-Retest methods (0.92) were used to examine the reliability of the inventory. The validity of the inventory has been established by adopting factorial and criterion related approach.

INSTRUCTIONS OF TESTS:

During the administration of the tests the following instructions were given to the respondents.

(1) Personality by H. J.Eysenck (M.P.I.):

इस प्रश्नावली में आपके व्यव्हार, भाव, कार्य आदि से सम्बंधित कुछ प्रश्न पूछे गए हैं। इन प्रश्नों के लिए कोई भी पूर्वनिश्चित "सही" या "गलत" उत्तर नहीं हो सकते हैं क्योंकि एक ही परिस्थिति में दो लोगो के अनुभव एवं विचार अलग अलग हो सकते हैं। अतः आप उसी उत्तर का चुनाव करें जो आपको सही लगे। हर प्रश्न के सामने तीन संभावित उत्तर दिए गए हैं: 'हाँ", "?" या "नहीं"। जो उत्तर आपके भाव को सही सही प्रकट करता है उसके सामने सही का निशान लगाना है पर यदि आप बिलकुल निश्चित न कर सके तो "?" के साथ खाने में निशान लगा सकते हैं।

जल्दी में यदि आप गलत खाने में निशान लगा दे तो उसे दो बार काट कर ठीक स्थान पर निशान लगायें। प्रश्नों का उत्तर देने में शीघ्रता करें। किसी भी प्रश्न को मत छोड़िये बल्कि हर एक प्रश्न का कुछ न कुछ उत्तर अवश्य दीजिये।

2. Adjustment Inventory by Sinha and Singh (1971):

जब तक आपसे कहा न जाये तब तक कोई पृष्ठ न पलटें । इस पुस्तिका पर कुछ न लिखें तथा इसका उपयोग सावधानी से करें जिससे इसका पुनः प्रयोग किया जा सके। इस पुस्तिका में कुछ कथन आपके व्यक्तित्व से सम्बंधित है तथा आपको अपने उत्तरों को अलग उत्तर सूची पर अंकित करना है। उत्तर सूची में प्रत्येक कथन के सामने "हाँ" एवं "ना" के दो खाने हैं। इन दोनों खानों में से आपको जो उपयुक्त लगे उस पर गोला बनाना है। आपके प्रत्युत्तरों को पूर्ण रूप से गुप्त रखा जायेगा इसलिए बिना संकोच के उत्तर दीजिये। यद्यपि समय की कोई सीमा नहीं है फिर भी आप कोशिश करें जितना शीघ्र हो सके काम समाप्त करें।

3. Achievement Motivation Inventory by V. P. Bhargava (1971):

आगे के पृष्ठों पर कुछ अधूरे वाक्य दिए गए है। इनमे से प्रत्येक के सामने तीन वैकल्पिक पूर्ति–वाक्य सुझाव के रूप में दिए गए हैं। आपको दिए हुए इन अधूरे वाक्यों की पूर्ति करने के लिए इनमे से किसी एक को, जिसे आप अपनी वर्तमान रुचि के अनुकूल एवं उपयुक्त समझते हैं, को चुनकर सही का निशान लगाना है। इस प्रकार आपको केवल एक ही वाक्यांश चुनकर अपनी राय देनी है। ध्यान रहे यहाँ कोई भी उत्तर सही या गलत नहीं है। आपको उत्तर अपनी वर्तमान स्तिथियों को सोचकर ही देना है। यदि कोई शंका हो तो पहले से पूछ लें। कार्य शीघ्रता से करें।

4. Emotional Intelligence

You are provided with a test booklet and an answer sheet. The front page of this booklet contains instructions and in the remaining pages there are 100 test statements for being responded as 'yes' or 'no'. All these statements are meant for knowing about the level of your emotional intelligence. There is no right or wrong answer to a question given in the booklet. After reading a particular question and considering what is appropriate for you, you have to simply respond to it as 'yes' or 'no'. It should be kept well in mind that you have not to write anything on the test booklet. It is simply a question paper. Answers are to be written on the answer sheet by putting a tick 'yes' or 'no' given against the serial no. of each statement. Try to provide free and frank responses without any fear and hesitation. Your responses will remain quite secret and confidential and may be used for the research purpose. Be careful that no statement should be left unanswered; otherwise you will not be having complete assessment of your emotional intelligence. There is no time limit for providing responses. However, you are requested to finish your work within 30 to 40 minutes. If you have any doubt, please ask.

ADMINISTRATION OF THE TESTS:

After selecting the respondents on the basis of information schedule, the tests were administered. First of all rapport was built with the respondents so that they responded to the questionnaires in relaxed state of mind. The respondents were assured that the information provided by them would be kept totally confidential and would be used only for the purpose of research. Simple and clear instructions printed on the questionnaires were read out and were explained to the respondents for each of the questionnaire. Then, investigator gave set of questionnaires to the respondents.

In between the answers given by respondents, it was checked whether the method of giving the answer was correct or not. In the end, they were asked to make sure that they had answered every question.

After the subjects completed the set of questionnaires, they were collected. Respondents were thanked for their co- operation extended during collection of data.

8. PROCEDURE:

After identifying and defining the problem as also accomplishing the relating tasks, following procedure was followed. In order to avoid inadequacies and flaws in the present study, pilot study was conducted which is then followed by the main study.

(A) PILOT STUDY

A pilot study was conducted with a view to pretest the tests and tools for the study so as to find out its suitability for being used in the present study. It was conducted over a sample of 30 respondents. Representatives of all the 6 experimental groups were taken in consideration. These respondents were other than those who were considered for the main study. Thus, on the basis of the pilot study, the sequence of administration of the all tests was determined. The pilot study also gave direction about the statistical procedures that could be used for final study.

(A) MAIN STUDY

The data from the sample of 180 respondents (which was divided in 6 groups as per the design of the study) were collected with the help of relevant and standardized tests. Data were collected from work place or home as per their convenience. Necessary precautions were taken as outlined in respective manuals with respect to administration and instructions.

SCORING:

Once the data had been collected, then the scoring of all the data was done according to the procedure laid down in the manual of different tests and tools. The raw scores were then computed and analyzed with suitable statistics.

9. STATISTICAL ANALYSIS:

The collected data from different sources were assembled together and scored according to the procedure given in the concerned manuals. The Raw scores were computed and were analyzed statistically. In order to obtain empirical verification of the proposed research, raw data was analyzed with the help of following statistical techniques.

Mean and Standard Deviation:

Mean, Standard Deviation (SD), SE and CV% of all the variables were computed with regard to personality, adjustment, achievement motivation and emotional intelligence.

Analysis of variance:

The main statistical technique used for the data was ANOVA to find out the main effect of the two independent variables on various dependent variables. Significance of the difference between means of various groups as per the independent variables was compared through ANOVA. Correlation was determined to find out the relationship between the dependent variables.

In order to illustrate data graphically, wherever necessary, Bar graphs were drawn.

CHAPTER - 4
RESULT AND DISCUSSION

Observation collected on the psychological variables have been statistically analyzed and presented under the following sections:

1. **Statistical summary of the observations:** It was prepared by calculating Mean, SD, SE and CV. The summary observation have been presented in tables A-1 to A-20.

2. **Analysis of Variance:** The observation on different parameters under study were subjected to ANOVA to study whether the average in respect of Six groups of subjects are significantly different or not. Analysis of variance of the parameters was studied separately for the six groups of subjects. The average values along with their SEm, CV and CD of different variables Personality, Adjustment, Achievement Motivation and Emotional intelligence in Table B-1 to B-5.

3. **Correlation studies:** The extent of linear association between the different variables under investigation was studied by Karl Pearson's Co-efficient of correlation. All the inter correlations between variables under investigation viz, Personality, Adjustment, Achievement Motivation and Emotional Intelligence were worked out using the raw score in case of individual respondents. The value of these inter correlation have been presented of Single adolescents belonging to low, moderate and high socio economic status and Sibling adolescents belonging to low, moderate and high socio economic group in table C-1 to C-12.

Statistical summary of the observation

The entire adolescents were divided into six groups viz single adolescents belonging to low socio economic status, Single adolescents belonging to moderate socio economic status, Single adolescents belonging to high socio economic status, Sibling adolescents belonging to low socio economic status, Sibling adolescents belonging to moderate socio economic status and Sibling adolescents belonging to high socio economic status. A sample of 180 from these six groups was selected for the purpose.
A summary of observation have been presented via tables A-1 to A-20.

SES – Socio Economic Status

Part- A

Table A-1

Statistical Summary of Neuroticism dimension of Personality in Adolescents

(Sample Size 30, Age-Group 13-18)

Group	Mean	SD	SE	CV%
Single Low SES	34.87	2.64	0.48	7.56
Single Moderate SES	38.17	2.25	0.41	5.88
Single High SES	30.33	2.67	0.49	8.80
Sibling Low SES	24.67	3.77	0.69	15.29
Sibling Moderate SES	19.20	2.47	0.45	12.86
Sibling High SES	16.33	2.32	0.42	14.23

Table A-1 indicates that there is difference in the mean score of neuroticism dimension of personality among all the groups. Single Low SES mean is 34.87, Single Moderate SES mean is 38.17, Single High SES mean is 30.33, Sibling Low SES mean is 24.67, Sibling Moderate SES mean is 19.20 and Sibling High SES mean is 16.33. It shows that single adolescents belonging to low, moderate and high socio economic status experience more neuroticism as compared to sibling adolescents belonging to same SES zones.

GRAPH: 4.1 GRAPHICAL PRESENTATION OF NEUROTICISM DIMENSION OF PERSONALITY

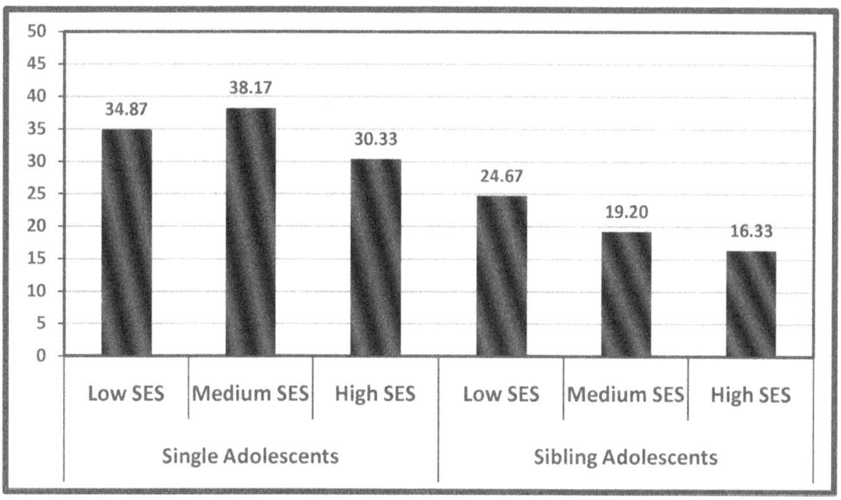

Table A-2

Statistical Summary of Extraversion dimension of Personality in Adolescents

(Sample Size 30, Age-Group 13-18)

Group	Mean	SD	SE	CV%
Single Low SES	18.37	3.29	0.60	17.89
Single Moderate SES	23.17	3.81	0.69	16.43
Single High SES	20.67	3.91	0.71	18.90
Sibling Low SES	35.57	3.23	0.59	9.09
Sibling Moderate SES	42.33	2.51	0.46	5.93
Sibling High SES	38.90	2.66	0.49	6.83

Table A-2 indicates that there is difference in the mean score of Extraversion dimension of personality among all the groups. Single Low SES mean is 18.37, Single Moderate SES mean is 23.17, Single High SES mean is 20.67, Sibling Low SES mean is 35.57, Sibling Moderate SES mean is 42.33 and Sibling High SES mean is 38.90. It shows that Sibling Adolescents belonging to low, moderate and high socio economic status scored high on extraversion as compared to single adolescents.

GRAPH: 4.2 GRAPHICAL PRESENTATION OF EXTRAVERSION DIMENSION OF PERSONALITY

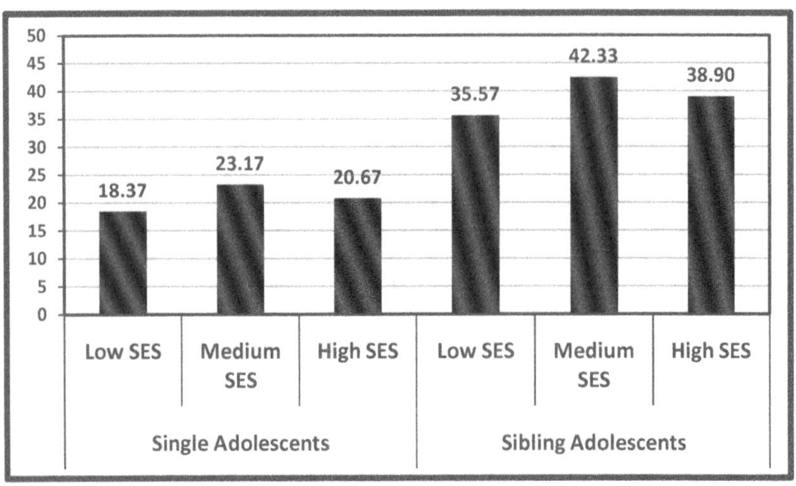

Table A-3
Statistical Summary of Adjustment in Adolescents
(Sample Size 30, Age-Group 13-18)

Group	Mean	SD	SE	CV%
Single Low SES	47.97	2.77	0.51	5.78
Single Moderate SES	44.07	2.78	0.51	6.31
Single High SES	46.17	4.62	0.84	10.00
Sibling Low SES	29.80	2.58	0.47	8.65
Sibling Moderate SES	25.80	2.92	0.53	11.31
Sibling High SES	28.40	3.93	0.72	13.83

The data presented in **Table A-3** describes that Adjustment Scores was higher (47.97) for Single Low SES as compared to that for Single Moderate SES (44.07) and Single High SES (46.17).The mean score of Sibling Low SES, Sibling Moderate SES and Sibling High SES were (29.80), (25.80) and (28.40) respectively. Higher mean score indicates poor adjustment. Hence the results clearly indicate that sibling adolescents show better adjustment than single adolescents.

GRAPH: 4.3 GRAPHICAL PRESENTATION OF ADJUSTMENT

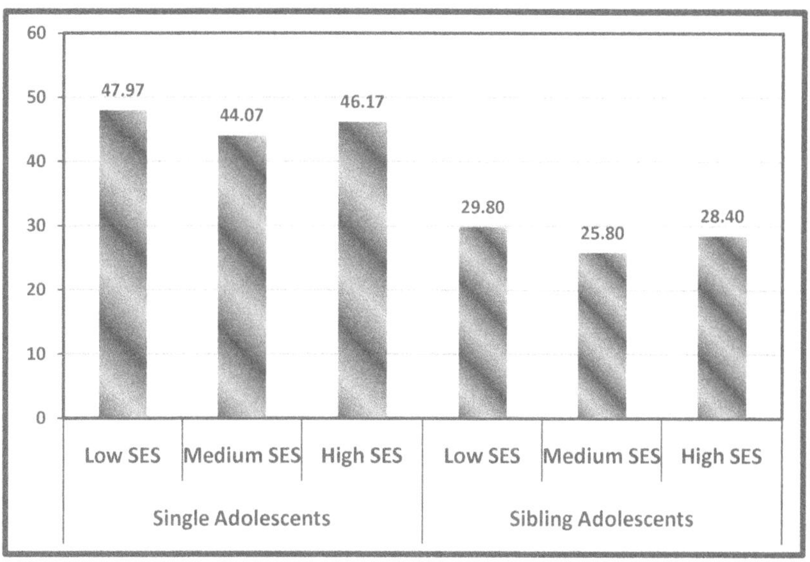

Table A-4
Statistical Summary of Achievement Motivation in Adolescents
(Sample Size 30, Age-Group 13-18)

Group	Mean	SD	SE	CV%
Single Low SES	14.00	1.64	0.30	11.71
Single Moderate SES	18.27	1.05	0.19	5.74
Single High SES	16.33	1.03	0.19	6.30
Sibling Low SES	18.23	1.14	0.21	6.23
Sibling Moderate SES	22.13	1.04	0.19	4.71
Sibling High SES	19.97	0.93	0.17	4.65

Table A-4 shows that achievement motivation Scores was higher (18.27) for Single Moderate SES as compared to that for Single Low SES (14.00) and Single High SES (16.33).The mean score of Sibling Low SES, Sibling Moderate SES and Sibling High SES were 18.23, 22.13 and 19.97 respectively. Sibling adolescents scored higher than single adolescents which show that they have high achievement motivation.

GRAPH: 4.4 GRAPHICAL PRESENTATION OF ACHIEVEMENT MOTIVATION

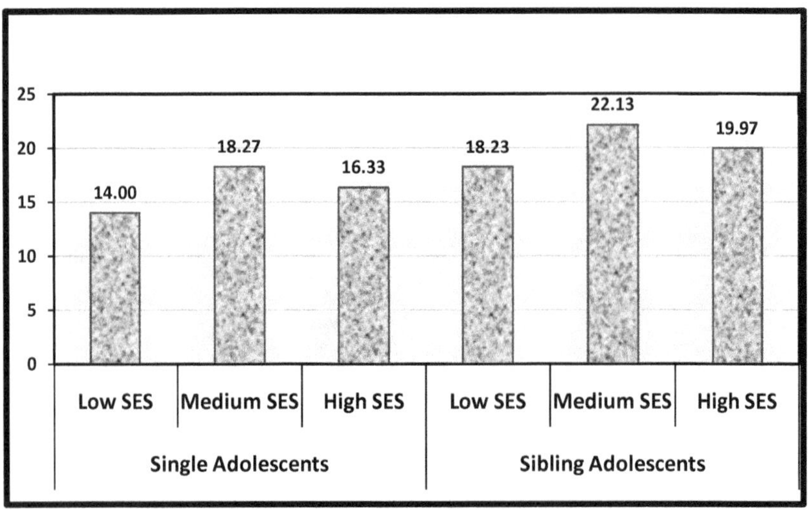

Table A-5
Statistical Summary of Emotional Intelligence in Adolescents
(Sample Size 30, Age-Group 13-18)

Group	Mean	SD	SE	CV%
Single Low SES	62.73	3.69	0.67	5.87
Single Moderate SES	77.93	2.00	0.36	2.56
Single High SES	70.07	1.34	0.24	1.91
Sibling Low SES	78.07	4.32	0.79	5.54
Sibling Moderate SES	91.87	2.05	0.37	2.23
Sibling High SES	84.00	2.20	0.40	2.62

Table A-5 indicates that there is difference in the mean score of Emotional Intelligence among all the groups. Single Low SES mean is 62.73, Single Moderate SES mean is 77.93, Single High SES mean is 70.07, Sibling Low SES mean is 78.07, Sibling Moderate SES mean is 91.87 and Sibling High SES mean is 84.00. Single Moderate SES mean (77.93) and Sibling Moderate SES mean (91.87) are highest than other Scores. It shows that the emotional intelligence of siblings is better than single adolescents.

GRAPH: 4.5 GRAPHICAL PRESENTATION OF EMOTIONAL INTELLIGENCE

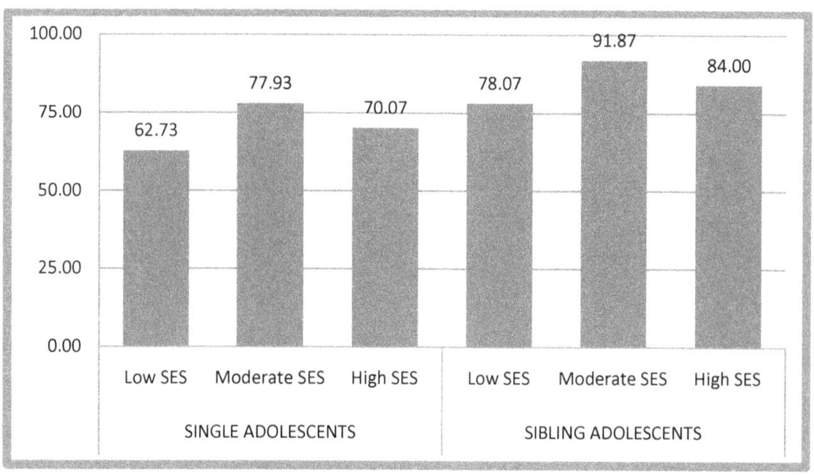

Table A-6

Statistical Summary of Neuroticism dimension of Personality on Type of Child
(Sample Size 90, Age Group 13-18)

Group	Mean	SD	SE	CV%
Single	34.46	4.08	0.41	11.84
Sibling	20.07	4.52	0.45	22.55

Table A-6 shows the mean score for neuroticism dimension of personality of single and sibling adolescents. According to table, mean value for single child is 34.46 and for sibling mean score is 20.07. Single child scored high on neuroticism dimension of personality as compared to the siblings. It shows high neurotic level of single adolescents.

Table A-7

Statistical Summary of Neuroticism dimension of Personality on Type of Socio Economic Status
(Sample Size 60, Age Group 13-18)

Group	Mean	SD	SE	CV%
Low	29.77	6.07	0.61	20.40
Moderate	28.68	9.85	0.98	34.32
High	23.33	7.48	0.75	32.07

It is obvious from the **Table A-7** that obtained mean score of neuroticism dimension of personality on Low SES is 29.77, Moderate SES is 28.68 and score on High SES is 23.33. It shows that there is difference in neurotic level of adolescents belonging to low, moderate and socio economic status.

Table A-8
Statistical Summary of Neuroticism dimension of Personality on Type of Overall Sample
(Sample Size 180, Age Group 13-18)

Group	Mean	SD	SE	CV%
Overall	27.26	8.40	0.84	30.80

Table A-8 indicates that the mean score of neuroticism dimension of personality for overall sample is 27.26, SD is 8.40, SE is 0.84 and CV is 30.80%.

Table A-9
Statistical Summary of Extraversion dimension of Personality on Type of Child
(Sample Size 90, Age Group 13-18)

Group	Mean	SD	SE	CV%
Single	20.73	4.13	0.41	19.94
Sibling	38.93	3.93	0.39	10.11

Table A-9 shows the mean score for Extraversion dimension of Personality of single and sibling adolescents. According to table, mean value for single child is 20.73 and for sibling mean score is 38.93. Sibling child scored high on Extraversion dimension of Personality as compared to the single child. It means that siblings are more extraverted as compared to single adolescents.

Table A-10

Statistical Summary of Extraversion dimension of Personality on Type of Socio Economic Status (Sample Size 60, Age Group 13-18)

Group	Mean	SD	SE	CV%
Low	26.97	9.26	0.93	34.32
Moderate	32.75	10.18	1.02	31.08
High	29.78	9.77	0.98	32.81

It is obvious from the **Table A-10** that obtained mean score of Extraversion dimension of Personality on Low SES is 26.97, Moderate SES is 32.75 and score on High SES is 29.78. It shows that adolescents belonging to moderate socio economic status are more extraverted than low and high socio economic status.

Table A-11

Statistical Summary of Extraversion dimension of Personality on Type of Overall Sample (Sample Size 180, Age Group 13-18)

Group	Mean	SD	SE	CV%
Overall	29.83	9.97	1.00	33.43

Table A-11 indicates that the mean score of Extraversion dimension of personality for overall sample is 29.83, SD is 9.97, SE is 1.00 and CV is 33.43%.

Table A-12

Statistical Summary of Adjustment on type of child
(Sample Size 90, Age-Group 13-18)

Group	Mean	SD	SE	CV%
Single	46.07	3.81	0.38	8.28
Sibling	28.00	3.57	0.36	12.75

Table A-12 shows the adjustment scores of single child and siblings. According to table, mean for single child is 46.07 and sibling child's adjustment mean score is 28.00. Single child scored high on adjustment as compared to the sibling child. The higher score indicates poor adjustment. Hence sibling adolescents show better adjustment than single adolescents.

Table A-13

Statistical Summary of Adjustment on type of Socio Economic Status
(Sample Size 60, Age-Group 13-18)

Group	Mean	SD	SE	CV%
Low	38.88	9.54	0.95	24.53
Moderate	34.93	9.63	0.96	27.58
High	37.28	9.92	0.99	26.59

It is obvious from the **Table A-13** that obtained mean score of adjustment on Low SES is 38.88, score of adjustment on the Moderate SES is 34.93 and score of adjustment on the High SES is 37.28. It shows that there is difference in the score of adolescents belonging to low, moderate and high socio economic status.

Table A-14

Statistical Summary of Adjustment on Type of Overall Sample (Sample Size 180, Age-Group 13-18)

Group	Mean	SD	SE	CV%
Overall	37.03	9.78	0.98	26.40

Table A-10 indicates that the adjustment mean score of overall sample is 37.03, SD is 9.78, SE is 0.98 and CV is 26.40%.

Table A-15

Statistical Summary of Achievement Motivation on Type of child (Sample Size 90, Age-Group 13-18)

Group	Mean	SD	SE	CV%
Single	16.20	2.16	0.22	13.32
Sibling	20.11	1.90	0.19	9.47

Table A-15 shows the mean score of achievement motivation on type of single and sibling adolescents. According to table, mean for single child is 16.20 and sibling child's achievement motivation mean score is 20.11. Sibling child scored high on achievement motivation as compared to the single child.

Table A-16

Statistical Summary of Achievement Motivation on Type of Socio Economic Status (Sample Size 60, Age-Group 13-18)

Group	Mean	SD	SE	CV%
Low	16.12	2.55	0.26	15.83
Moderate	20.20	2.21	0.22	10.93
High	18.15	2.07	0.21	11.42

Table A-16 shows that score of achievement motivation on Low SES is 16.12, score of achievement motivation on the Moderate SES is 20.20 and score of achievement motivation on the High SES is 18.15. It shows that Moderate SES score is the highest among others.

Table A-17

Statistical Summary of Achievement Motivation on type of Overall Sample (Sample Size 180, Age-Group 13-18)

Group	Mean	SD	SE	CV%
Overall	18.16	2.82	0.28	15.54

Table A-17 indicates that the achievement motivation mean score of overall sample is 18.16, SD is 2.82, SE is 0.28 and CV is 15.54%.

Table A-18

Statistical Summary of Emotional Intelligence on Type of Child (Sample Size 90, Age-Group 13-18)

Group	Mean	SD	SE	CV%
Single	70.24	6.73	0.67	9.58
Sibling	84.64	6.43	0.64	7.60

Table A-18 reflects the mean score of Emotional Intelligence on type of single child and sibling child. According to table, mean for single child is 70.24 and sibling child's Emotional Intelligence mean score is 84.64. Sibling child scored high on Emotional Intelligence as compared to the single child.

Table A-19

Statistical Summary of Emotional Intelligence on Type of Socio Economic Status (Sample Size 60, Age-Group 13-18)

Group	Mean	SD	SE	CV%
Low	70.40	8.70	0.87	12.35
Moderate	84.90	7.31	0.73	8.61
High	77.03	7.25	0.73	9.42

Table A-19 results indicate that score of Emotional Intelligence on Low SES is 70.40, score of Emotional Intelligence on the Moderate SES is 84.90 and score of Emotional Intelligence on the High SES is 77.03. It shows that Moderate SES score is the highest among others.

Table A-20

Statistical Summary of Emotional Intelligence on Type of Overall Sample (Sample Size 180, Age-Group 13-18)

Group	Mean	SD	SE	CV%
Overall	77.44	7.71	0.77	9.95

In **Table A-20** the variable Emotional Intelligence mean score of overall sample is 77.44, SD is 7.71, SE is 0.77 and CV is 9.95%.

Part B
Analysis of Variance
Table B-1
F-ratio for Neuroticism level of different groups of subjects along with their SEm, CD and CV values.

Scource	DF	SS	MS	Fcal
Groups	5	11320.29	2264.06	302.93**
Error	174	1300.43	7.47	
Total	179	12620.73		
SEM	0.39			
CD 5%	1.07			
CD 1%	1.41			
CV %	9.29			

***Significant at the level of 0.01*

A significant difference in F ratio for Neuroticism dimension of Personality has been observed between different groups of subjects at 1% level of significance. So the null hypothesis 1 & 5 are rejected here.

As indicated from Table (A-1, A-6 and A-7) there is difference in the mean score of neuroticism dimension of personality among all the groups. Single adolescents scored higher (34.46) on neuroticism level as compared to sibling adolescents (20.07). On the other hand, based on socio economic status, adolescents belonging to low socio economic status (29.77) scored high as compared to adolescents from moderate (28.68) and high socio economic status (23.33). It indicates that neurotic level of adolescents belonging to low socio economic status is higher than adolescents from moderate and high socio economic status.

There might be many reasons for the observed difference. Single adolescents sometimes may lack control over their life whereas sibling adolescents are considered to be calm and collected most of the time. Sibling adolescents also have a strong sense of self and feel that they are in control of their world. Single adolescents may also experience feelings like anxiety, anger, guilt and depression because they don't have access to resources needed for their overall development. This may lead to many health issues. In order to deal with chronic stress and anxiety they may adapt maladaptive coping strategies. Single adolescents respond badly to environmental stress and take ordinary situations as threatening. In contrast, adolescents with siblings can easily deal with feelings like anxiety, anger, guilt and depression as they have their brother or sister to share their joys and sorrows and to solve difficulties aroused. Sibling adolescents are also able to understand and interpret the environmental situations that they come across and face them confidently. These outcomes are also supported by the study of **Gupta (2017),** who explored the personality traits of different birth orders and found that there was a significant difference between different birth orders on personality traits.

Socio economic status refers to ranking of an individual by the society he lives in terms of his material belongings and cultural possessions along with the degree of respect, power and influence. Socioeconomic status has long been known as a good predictor of academic achievement. Many researchers have demonstrated the importance of the relationship between family background and student achievement. Many studies were conducted in relationship of socio economic status and academic achievement. Students come from very different socio-economic classes, values, intelligence, capacity and ideas. The mean scores indicated that adolescents belonging to low Socio Economic Status (SES) have high level of neuroticism as compared to adolescents belonging to moderate and high SES zone. There might be many reasons for this difference. Adolescents spending their lives in low SES are more likely to experience poorer health than those who spend their lives in moderate and high SES. There is found greater prevalence of negative personality pattern in adolescents from low SES. Higher hostility in adolescents belonging to low SES may also lead to poor psychosocial functioning. The adolescents from low SES show maladaptive coping behaviors. They can't effectively deal with chronic stress. Adolescents from low SES experience anxiety, depression and hostility as they can't fulfill all their desires which they want to. Whereas adolescents belonging to moderate and high SES have an easy access to many of the things they need to fulfill their desires, hence they don't experience anxiety and hostility. Similar results were also found in the study of **Sweeting, and Hunt (2014)**. They also found that lower SES was associated with increased physical symptoms, psychological distress and anxiety. The results are also supported by the study of **Jonassaint, et al. (2011).** They found that low SES was associated with high neuroticism and low conscientiousness.

Table B-2

F-ratio for Extraversion level of different groups of subjects along with their SEm, CD and CV values.

Scource	DF	SS	MS	Fcal
Groups	5	15938.47	3187.69	297.16**
Error	174	1866.53	10.73	
Total	179	17805.00		
SEM	0.46			
CD 5%	1.28			
CD 1%	1.68			
CV %	10.17			

***Significant at the level of 0.01*

A significant difference in F ratio for Extraversion dimension of Personality has been observed between different groups of subjects at 1% level of significance. So the null hypothesis 1 & 5 are rejected here.

As indicated from Table (A-2, A-9 and A-10) there is difference in the mean score of extraversion dimension of personality among all the groups. Sibling adolescents (38.93) scored higher on extraversion level as compared to single adolescents (20.73). On the other hand, based on socio economic status, adolescents belonging to moderate socio economic status (32.75) scored high as compared to adolescents from low (26.97) and high socio economic status (29.78). It indicates that adolescents from moderate socio economic status are more extraverted than adolescents from low and high socio economic status.

Siblings are considered to be more extraverted as compared to single child. They exhibit high desire for interpersonal interaction. However, the only child on the other hand shall find difficulties to interact in an effective way. Sometimes circumstances doesn't allow sharing difficulties with guardians, and particularly in this scenario sibling adolescents shall easily face this challenge as they could share their feelings with their brother or sister whom they trust enough to seek help, however, single adolescents shall find it hard enough to counter such challenges. These results are supported by the study of **Stephen, et al. (2017)** who investigated the relationship between sibling birth spacing and, extroversion and introversion characteristics of adolescents and concluded that close sibling spacing produces extraverted and highly aggressive children while wide sibling spacing produces introverted and less aggressive children. Their study further found that the only children, ranked highest in introversion and, lowest in aggressiveness and extraversion.

Only child and siblings differ in terms of sharing stuffs. Only child doesn't like to share anything with anyone. On the other hand, siblings like to share things with others. Another difference between being only raised and having siblings is relationship with their family. Siblings always have companions and playmates. They can play together, learn together, have conversation, and share their problems with one another. Also, they can learn from their elder siblings or teach their younger ones. They also help to take care of each other. The older sibling can help the younger sibling to learn how to live with others, help with homework, etc. In contrary, an only child receives more attention from his parents. Their parents help them in completing homework. The only child enjoys more time to spend with mom or dad, and perhaps more or better toys, clothes, etc.

The absence of siblings and the closeness with adults may interfere in the intellectual and personality development. Some people also believe that only-children receive excessive attention, mature precociously and, due to the absence of siblings, become selfish, demanding, dependent and moody, in comparison to children with siblings.

The study also reveals the difference in the mean score of adolescents belonging to different socio economic status. The mean scores indicated that adolescents from moderate socio economic status are more extraverted than adolescent from low and high socio economic status. Families with moderate socioeconomic status provide better facilities for the all round development to their children as they have easy access to wide range of resources. They also impart high quality care, books and toys to encourage them in various learning activities. The parents of high socio economic status also provide the same facilities but the adolescents from such families may misuse these facilities by enjoying parties, outing, watching movies etc. Whereas the parents belonging to low socio economic status are not able to provide all the required facilities to their children as they suffer from financial burden. The parents from moderate socio economic status easily get information regarding their children's health, as well as their emotional, social and cognitive development. That is why the adolescents from moderate socio economic status are more extraverted than adolescents from low and high socio economic status.

Table B-3

F-ratio for Adjustment of different groups of subjects along with their SEm, CD and CV values.

Scource	DF	SS	MS	Fcal
Groups	5	15164.00	3032.80	270.37**
Error	174	1951.80	11.22	
Total	179	17115.80		
SEM	0.47			
CD 5%	1.31			
CD 1%	1.72			
CV %	10.29			

***Significant at the level of 0.01*

A significant difference in F ratio for adjustment has been observed between different groups of subjects at 1% level of significance. So the null hypothesis 2 & 6 are rejected here.

As indicated from Table (A-3, A-12 and A-13) there is difference in the mean score of adjustment among all the groups. Single adolescents (46.07) scored higher on adjustment as compared to sibling adolescents (28.00). As the higher score indicates poor adjustment, therefore sibling adolescents who scored low are considered to show better adjustment. On the other hand, based on socio economic status, adolescents belonging to low socio economic status (38.88) and high socio economic status (37.28) scored high as compared to adolescents from moderate (34.93) socio economic status. It indicates that the adjustment of moderate socio economic status is better than adolescents from low and high socio economic status.

It is well known that adolescence is a time for change as the young person faces many new experiences. Depending on the cultural contexts, the various environments in which the adolescent moves are likely to present new and unexpected situations that require responses that the adolescent may have never previously used. Dealing with the unexpected and being required to use new untested responses is likely to raise anxiety and cause stress in the young person. The period of adolescence is the most critical period of individual's life. In this period equilibrium of physical, mental and social forces is lost, and the result is that the individual has to make new adjustments with his own self, with the family and with the society at large. Therefore adjustment to various situations is considered to be a challenge for adolescents they are supposed to deal with.

The term adjustment refers to a degree to which an individual's personality functions efficiently in the world of people. It refers to the harmonious relationship between the person and the environment. A well adjusted personality can efficiently and effectively play the roles which are expected to him within given environment. His needs are satisfied according to social needs. Adjustment means the response to the demands and pressures of social environment forced upon the individual.

Sibling relationship is a long lasting relationship that a person has during his life time. Closeness may be the dimension of sibling relationships that acts as a protective and enduring factor. Sibling relationship is an emotionally intense type of relationship where they share their feelings with one another. Additionally, sibling adolescents understand the joy of sharing with others. However, single child on the other hand shall find it challenging to easily mingle with others. They usually dominate others which may lead to lot of problems, especially adjustment problems. Due to absence of siblings they become dependent, selfish, demanding and moody. Being an only child affect their personality development, social and emotional development and intellectual development. Siblings always have companions and playmates. They can play together, learn together, have conversation, and share their problems with one another. Also, they can learn from their elder siblings or teach their younger ones. They also help to take care of each other. These characteristics associated with the sibling child develop better adjustment than single child. Social adjustment is also of great importance at the period of adolescence due to an increasing relationship between adolescents and their peers at this period of life. Siblings are well adjusted and show low level of loneliness. They receive higher level of social support in their lives. They show healthy adjustment in school, family and society as compared to only child. They receive empathy from their parents as well as from their brothers and sisters which help to reduce their stress. An only child does not have any brother or sister, shall lack academic, emotional and social support because he has fewer tendencies to share his feelings. In most societies, siblings usually grow up together to develop strong emotional bonds such as love, or thoughtfulness. The emotional relationship between siblings is greatly influenced by parental treatment, birth order, personality, and personal experiences inside and outside the family. Brothers or sisters can be a source of companionship, help or emotional support. Older siblings serve as caretakers, teachers or models; in some situations they can even help compensate for absent or distant parents. In their interactions with each other, siblings acquire many social and cognitive skills which lead to healthy social development. The results are supported by the study of **Bahreasemani, et al. (2015).** They studied to compare social adjustment, self-worthiness and achievement motivation among only- child adolescence and adolescence with sibling. The results revealed that there was a significant difference between both groups of adolescence in social adjustment.

Socio economic background also influences adjustments in adolescents. The adjustment of adolescents from moderate socio economic status is better than adolescents belonging to low and high socio economic status. The parents from moderate socio economic status can provide financial, educational and social support and also provide facilities like proper nutritious food for their children's physical growth and better assistance in academics through good schools, teachers and counseling facilities etc. for mental competition but adolescents from low socio economic status lack these facilities due to which their educational, social and emotional adjustment gets affected. The adolescents from high socio economic status also have easy access to all the resources but sometimes they start misusing them which may lead to adjustment problems.

Table B-4

F-ratio for Achievement Motivation of different groups of subjects along with their SEm, CD and CV values.

Scource	DF	SS	MS	Fcal
Groups	5	1191.31	238.26	176.92**
Error	174	234.33	1.35	
Total	179	1425.64		
SEM	0.16			
CD 5%	0.45			
CD 1%	0.60			
CV %	6.06			

***Significant at the level of 0.01*

A significant difference in F ratio for achievement motivation has been observed between different groups of subjects at 1% level of significance. So the null hypothesis 3 & 7 are rejected here.

As indicated from Table (A-4, A-15 and A-16) there is difference in the mean score of achievement motivation among all the groups. Sibling adolescents (20.11) scored higher on achievement motivation as compared to single adolescents (16.20). On the other hand, based on socio economic status, adolescents belonging to moderate socio economic status (20.20) scored high as compared to adolescents from low (16.12) and high (18.15) socio economic status. It indicates that adolescents from moderate socio economic status show better achievement motivation than adolescents from low and high socio economic status.

Achievement motivation refers to the desire of a person to meet certain standards of excellence. It is not biological but shows a tremendous effect on human behavior. People differ in the degree to which they experience this need. It is acquired by children during the formative stages of social development. They learn it from their parents and socio-cultural environment. They acquire the values that they should attain a good position, social standing and distinguished status in the society.

The sibling child learn to develop achievement motivation by observing their siblings or get motivated and supported by them to earn the same. In contrast the single child does not have the competition of acquiring better position or social standing. Older siblings play a vital role in motivating or discouraging the achievement of younger siblings. Older siblings also help in setting up plans for high achievement. The interaction between older and younger sibling help younger ones to develop new experiences, communication skills, social skills and problem solving strategies etc. The older sibling acts as working model for enhancing the achievement of younger ones. Academic skills of older siblings influence the academic outcomes of younger ones. They also help in reducing the stress and negative impact of failure. As the children spend large amount of time with their siblings, so experience of interaction with siblings help in social and emotional development of their younger siblings. Therefore sibling relationships across early, middle and late adolescence continue to play an important role in adolescents' lives. Adolescents feel that they are more respected and understood by their siblings. They can share their views and opinions easily with their siblings, and are more open towards understanding others opinions. Adolescents also feel more comfortable to seek any help related to academics from their siblings while sometimes they feel hesitated to ask for the same to their parents. The results are supported by the study of **Dagys Pajoluk (2013)** who found that during adolescence older siblings serve as examples for younger ones. The goal of their study was to determine whether older sibling support enhances the academic achievement of younger ones. The results of this study provided support that older siblings' academic engagement is a key aspect of older sibling support that relates to younger siblings' academic achievement. This study highlighted the importance of both sibling and family variables in influencing younger siblings' achievement. Similar results were also obtained by the study of **Ryherd (2011).** He tried to understand the relationship between an adolescent's older sibling and peers on their academic achievement. The warmth and support level of positive older siblings to the peers and their academic achievement was measured in this study. The results of this study revealed that positive warmth and support from an older sibling directly influenced an adolescent's academic achievement.

Socio economic background also influences achievement motivation in adolescents. Families with moderate socioeconomic status provide better facilities than low socio-economic status. They also have better access to the resources need to achieve their goals. The parents of moderate socio economic status can easily get information about their children's interest, strength as well as their emotional, social and cognitive development. The children from moderate socioeconomic status attend school on regular basis and enjoy better educational outcomes than adolescents belonging to low socioeconomic status. The adolescents belonging to low socioeconomic status do not get opportunity to attend the school on regular basis as their parents send them for work due to financial instability. This is the main reason behind the decline of educational outcomes of these children. Although the adolescents from high socio economic status also receive all the resources and facilities from their parents but they may misuse them by spending money unnecessarily in parties and other activities. Although their parents provide them financial support but if these children don't get motivated by their parents due to their busy schedule they feel low and dissatisfied.

Table B-5

F-ratio for Emotional Intelligence of different groups of subjects along with their SEm, CD and CV values.

Scource	DF	SS	MS	Fcal
Groups	5	1191.31	238.26	176.92
Error	174	234.33	1.35	
Total	179	1425.64		
SEM	0.16			
CD 5%	0.45			
CD 1%	0.60			
CV %	6.06			

***Significant at the level of 0.01*

A significant difference in F ratio for emotional intelligence has been observed between different groups of subjects at 1% level of significance. So the null hypothesis 4 & 8 are rejected here.

As indicated from Table (A-4, A-18 and A-19) there is difference in the mean score of emotional intelligence among all the groups. Sibling adolescents (84.64) scored higher on emotional intelligence as compared to single adolescents (70.24). It indicates that emotional intelligence of sibling adolescents is better than single adolescents. On the other hand, based on socio economic status, adolescents belonging to moderate socio economic status (84.90) scored high on emotional intelligence as compared to adolescents from low (70.40) and high socio economic status (77.03). It indicates that emotional intelligence of adolescents from moderate socio economic status was better than adolescents from low and high socio economic status.

Emotional intelligence means the capability of a person to manage and control his emotions and the emotions of others as well. It is the ability to identify and manage emotions of self and the emotions of others. In most societies, siblings usually grow up together to develop strong emotional bonds such as love, or thoughtfulness. The emotional relationship between siblings is greatly influenced by parental treatment, birth order, personality, and personal experiences inside and outside the family. Brothers or sisters can be a source of companionship, help or emotional support. Older siblings serve as caretakers, teachers or models; in some situations they can even help compensate for absent or distant parents. These characteristics of the sibling child help them to grow self awareness, self regulation, motivation, empathy and social skills that increases their Emotional Intelligence than the single child who doesn't have or less experience to deal with the other individuals or society. Sibling children interact with each other and acquire many social and cognitive skills which lead to healthy social development.

For any child, family is an initial yet very important place wherein he learns how to maintain a good relationship with the siblings and other family members. The elder sibling helps younger ones to develop moral values. With the assistance of older siblings younger children learn to become kind and responsible. They also learn to handle stress in diverse and difficult situations. While imitating the older sibling younger one also learn to manage their feelings and express their emotions in a particular situation. The habit of controlling emotions is also developed in them. So the children having siblings are more open and carry experience to resolve their conflicts easily than single child. In contrast to this only child grows up without siblings, hence he finds difficulty in understanding the feelings and emotions of others. As they find challenging to manage and control their emotions, they may be anxious and frightened to deal with difficult circumstances. Similar results were found in the study of **Ghanawat, et al. (2016)** who assessed the relationship between family functioning and emotional intelligence among adolescents. They found a significant positive correlation between family functioning and emotional intelligence. They also found that healthy family relationship help in developing better emotional intelligence.

The economic condition of the family also plays an important role in determining the way adolescents handle any situation or relationship. These conditions affect the way, these children think, empathize and their ability to deal with stress. The mean scores indicated that emotional intelligence of adolescents belonging to moderate socio economic status is better than adolescents from low and high socio economic status. The adolescents belonging to moderate socioeconomic status have easy access to resources necessary for their overall development than adolescents from low socio economic status. Due to availability of all resources these children gain better education and exposure. They get better opportunities to develop emotional learning and eventually they become more emotionally intelligent. Although the adolescents from high socio economic status also receive everything they require from their parents but their overconfidence may lead to misuse of money and hence affect their personality development. Although the parents from high class provide financial support to their children but they don't have enough time to give them emotional support.

Part C
Correlation

Table C-1

Inter correlation matrix of different psychological parameter in single and sibling adolescents.
(Sample Size 180, Age-Group 13-18)

	Neuroticism	Extraversion	Adjustment	Achievement Motivation	Emotional Intelligence
Neuroticism	1.00	0.42**	0.06	0.23**	-0.19**
Extraversion		1.00	0.11	0.31**	0.34**
Adjustment			1.00	0.09	-0.06
Achievement Motivation				1.00	0.23**
Emotional Intelligence					1.00

**Significant at the level of 0.05*
***Significant at the level of 0.01*

Table C-1 depicts that Neuroticism was having positive association with Extraversion (r=0.42), Adjustment (r=0.06) and Achievement Motivation (r=0.23) where as negative association with Emotional Intelligence (r=-0.19). Extraversion was found to have positive association with Adjustment (r=0.11), Achievement Motivation (r=0.31) and Emotional Intelligence (0.34). Adjustment was having positive association with achievement motivation (r=0.09) and negative association with Emotional Intelligence (r=-0.06). Achievement Motivation was having positive association with Emotional Intelligence (r=0.23).

Table C-2

Inter correlation matrix of different psychological parameter in single adolescents. (Sample Size 90, Age-Group 13-18)

	Neuroticism	Extraversion	Adjustment	Achievement Motivation	Emotional Intelligence
Neuroticism	1.00	-0.38**	-0.13	-0.06	-0.26**
Extraversion		1.00	0.19**	0.24**	0.31**
Adjustment			1.00	0.03	0.41**
Achievement Motivation				1.00	0.34**
Emotional Intelligence					1.00

**Significant at the level of 0.05*
***Significant at the level of 0.01*

Table C-2 depicts that Neuroticism was having negative association with Extraversion (r=-0.38), Adjustment (r=-0.13), Achievement Motivation (r=-0.06) and Emotional Intelligence (r=-0.26). Extraversion was found to have positive association with Adjustment (r=0.19), Achievement Motivation (r=0.24) and Emotional Intelligence (0.31). Adjustment was having positive association with Achievement Motivation (r=0.03) and Emotional Intelligence (r=0.41). Achievement Motivation was having positive association with Emotional Intelligence (r=0.34).

Table C-3
Inter correlation matrix of different psychological parameters in sibling adolescents.
(Sample Size 90, Age-Group 13-18)
Correlation Table of (Sibling)

	Neuroticism	Extraversion	Adjustment	Achievement Motivation	Emotional Intelligence
Neuroticism	1.00	0.06	0.23**	0.43**	0.05
Extraversion		1.00	-0.14*	-0.16*	0.45**
Adjustment			1.00	0.09	0.23**
Achievement Motivation				1.00	0.11
Emotional Intelligence					1.00

**Significant at the level of 0.05*
***Significant at the level of 0.01*

Table C-3 depicts that Neuroticism was having positive association with Extraversion (r=0.06), Adjustment (r=-0.23), Achievement Motivation (r=0.43) and Emotional Intelligence (r=0.05). Extraversion was found to have negative association with Adjustment (r=-0.14), Achievement Motivation (r=-0.16) and positive association with Emotional Intelligence (0.45). Adjustment was having positive association with Achievement Motivation (r=0.09) and Emotional Intelligence (r=0.23). Achievement Motivation was having positive association with Emotional Intelligence (r=0.11).

Table C-4

Inter correlation matrix of different psychological parameter Low SES in overall. (Sample Size 60, Age-Group 13-18)

	Neuroticism	Extraversion	Adjustment	Achievement Motivation	Emotional Intelligence
Neuroticism	1.00	0.54**	-0.06	0.15*	0.11
Extraversion		1.00	0.00	0.29**	0.43**
Adjustment			1.00	0.13	0.34**
Achievement Motivation				1.00	0.51**
Emotional Intelligence					1.00

**Significant at the level of 0.05*
***Significant at the level of 0.01*

Table C-4 depicts that Neuroticism was having positive association with Extraversion (r=0.54), Achievement Motivation (r=0.15) and Emotional Intelligence (r=0.11) whereas negative association with Adjustment (r=-0.06). Extraversion was found to have no association with Adjustment whereas positive association with Achievement Motivation (r=0.29) and Emotional Intelligence (0.43). Adjustment was having positive association with Achievement Motivation (r=0.13) and Emotional Intelligence (r=0.34). Achievement Motivation was having positive association with Emotional Intelligence (r=0.51).

Table C-5

Inter correlation matrix of different psychological parameter Moderate SES in overall.
(Sample Size 60, Age-Group 13-18)

	Neuroticism	Extraversion	Adjustment	Achievement Motivation	Emotional Intelligence
Neuroticism	1.00	0.34**	0.09	0.14*	0.31**
Extraversion		1.00	-0.02	0.43**	0.07
Adjustment			1.00	-0.17*	0.02
Achievement Motivation				1.00	0.31**
Emotional Intelligence					1.00

**Significant at the level of 0.05*
***Significant at the level of 0.01*

Table C-5 depicts that Neuroticism was having positive association with Extraversion (r=0.34), Adjustment (r=0.09), Achievement Motivation (r=0.14) and Emotional Intelligence (r=0.31). Extraversion was found to have negative association with Adjustment (r=-0.02) whereas positive association with Achievement Motivation (r=0.43) and Emotional Intelligence (0.07). Adjustment was having positive association with Emotional Intelligence (r=0.02) and negative association with Achievement Motivation (r=-0.17). Achievement Motivation was having positive association with Emotional Intelligence (r=0.31).

Table C-6

Inter correlation matrix of different psychological parameter High SES in overall. (Sample Size 60, Age-Group 13-18)

	Neuroticism	Extraversion	Adjustment	Achievement Motivation	Emotional Intelligence
Neuroticism	1.00	-0.42**	-0.35**	0.02	-0.12
Extraversion		1.00	0.21**	-0.02	0.04
Adjustment			1.00	0.19**	0.37**
Achievement Motivation				1.00	0.39**
Emotional Intelligence					1.00

**Significant at the level of 0.05*
***Significant at the level of 0.01*

Table C-1 depicts that Neuroticism was having negative association with Extraversion (r=-0.42), Adjustment (r=-0.35) and Emotional Intelligence (r=-0.12) whereas positive association with Achievement Motivation (r=0.02). Extraversion was found to have positive association with Adjustment (r=0.21) and Emotional Intelligence (0.04) whereas negative association with Achievement Motivation (r=-0.02). Adjustment was having positive association with Achievement Motivation (r=0.19) and Emotional Intelligence (r=0.37). Achievement Motivation was having positive association with Emotional Intelligence (r=0.39).

Table C-7

Inter correlation matrix of different psychological parameter Low SES in Single. (Sample Size 30, Age-Group 13-18)

	Neuroticism	Extraversion	Adjustment	Achievement Motivation	Emotional Intelligence
Neuroticism	1.00	-0.17*	-0.18**	-0.22**	-0.07
Extraversion		1.00	0.13	0.28**	0.29**
Adjustment			1.00	0.11	0.42**
Achievement Motivation				1.00	0.36**
Emotional Intelligence					1.00

**Significant at the level of 0.05*
***Significant at the level of 0.01*

Table C-7 depicts that Neuroticism was having negative association with Extraversion (r=-0.17), Adjustment (r=-0.18) and Achievement Motivation (r=-0.22) and Emotional Intelligence (r=-0.07). Extraversion was found to have positive association with Adjustment (r=0.13), Achievement Motivation (r=0.28) and Emotional Intelligence (0.29). Adjustment was having positive association with Achievement Motivation (r=0.11) and Emotional Intelligence (r=0.42). Achievement Motivation was having positive association with Emotional Intelligence (r=0.36).

Table C-8

Inter correlation matrix of different psychological parameter Low SES in Siblings. (Sample Size 30, Age-Group 13-18)

	Neuroticism	Extraversion	Adjustment	Achievement Motivation	Emotional Intelligence
Neuroticism	1.00	0.10	-0.01	0.24**	0.26**
Extraversion		1.00	0.06	-0.07	0.34**
Adjustment			1.00	0.08	0.19**
Achievement Motivation				1.00	0.48**
Emotional Intelligence					1.00

**Significant at the level of 0.05*
***Significant at the level of 0.01*

Table C-8 depicts that Neuroticism was having positive association with Extraversion (r=0.10), Achievement Motivation (r=0.24) and Emotional Intelligence (r=0.26) where as negative association with Adjustment (r=-0.01). Extraversion was found to have positive association with Adjustment (r=0.06) and Emotional Intelligence (0.34) whereas negative association with Achievement Motivation (r=-0.07). Adjustment was having positive association with Achievement Motivation (r=0.08) and Emotional Intelligence (r=0.19). Achievement Motivation was having positive association with Emotional Intelligence (r=0.48).

Table C-9

Inter correlation matrix of different psychological parameter Moderate SES in single. (Sample Size 30, Age-Group 13-18)

	Neuroticism	Extraversion	Adjustment	Achievement Motivation	Emotional Intelligence
Neuroticism	1.00	0.01	0.00	0.14*	0.33**
Extraversion		1.00	0.01	0.05	0.11
Adjustment			1.00	-0.12	-0.09
Achievement Motivation				1.00	0.39**
Emotional Intelligence					1.00

**Significant at the level of 0.05*
***Significant at the level of 0.01*

Table C-9 depicts that Neuroticism was having positive association with Extraversion (r=0.01), Achievement Motivation (r=0.14) and Emotional Intelligence (r=0.33) whereas no association with Adjustment. Extraversion was found to have positive association with Adjustment (r=0.01), Achievement Motivation (r=0.05) and Emotional Intelligence (0.11). Adjustment was having negative association with Achievement Motivation (r=-0.12) and Emotional Intelligence (r=-0.09). Achievement Motivation was having positive association with Emotional Intelligence (r=0.39).

Table C-10

Inter correlation matrix of different psychological parameter Moderate SES in Siblings.
(Sample Size 30, Age-Group 13-18)

	Neuroticism	Extraversion	Adjustment	Achievement Motivation	Emotional Intelligence
Neuroticism	1.00	0.15*	0.10	0.16*	0.05
Extraversion		1.00	-0.18**	0.06	0.15*
Adjustment			1.00	-0.04	0.08
Achievement Motivation				1.00	-0.07
Emotional Intelligence					1.00

**Significant at the level of 0.05*
***Significant at the level of 0.01*

Table C-10 depicts that Neuroticism was having positive association with Extraversion (r=0.15), Adjustment (r=0.10).Achievement Motivation (r=0.16) and Emotional Intelligence (r=0.05). Extraversion was found to have negative association with Adjustment (r=-0.18) whereas positive association with Achievement Motivation (r=0.06) and Emotional Intelligence (0.15). Adjustment was having negative association with Achievement Motivation (r=-0.04) whereas positive association with Emotional Intelligence (r=0.08). Achievement Motivation was having negative association with Emotional Intelligence (r=-0.07).

Table C-11

Inter correlation matrix of different psychological parameter High SES in Single. (Sample Size 30, Age-Group 13-18)

	Neuroticism	Extraversion	Adjustment	Achievement Motivation	Emotional Intelligence
Neuroticism	1.00	-0.44**	-0.26**	0.13	0.04
Extraversion		1.00	0.25**	0.18**	0.00
Adjustment			1.00	0.09	0.38**
Achievement Motivation				1.00	0.51**
Emotional Intelligence					1.00

**Significant at the level of 0.05*
***Significant at the level of 0.01*

Table C-11 depicts that Neuroticism was having positive association with Achievement Motivation (r=0.13) and Emotional Intelligence (r=0.04) whereas negative association with Extraversion (r=-0.44) and Adjustment (r=-0.26). Extraversion was found to have positive association with Adjustment (r=0.25) and Achievement Motivation (r=0.18) whereas no association with Emotional Intelligence. Adjustment was having positive association with Achievement Motivation (r=0.09) and Emotional Intelligence (r=0.38). Achievement Motivation was having positive association with Emotional Intelligence (r=0.51).

Table C-12

Inter correlation matrix of different psychological parameter High SES in Siblings. (Sample Size 30, Age-Group 13-18)

	Neuroticism	Extraversion	Adjustment	Achievement Motivation	Emotional Intelligence
Neuroticism	1.00	-0.13	-0.15*	-0.07	-0.24**
Extraversion		1.00	-0.18**	-0.10	0.22**
Adjustment			1.00	0.13	0.10
Achievement Motivation				1.00	0.20**
Emotional Intelligence					1.00

**Significant at the level of 0.05*
***Significant at the level of 0.01*

Table C-12 depicts that Neuroticism was having negative association with Extraversion (r=-0.13), Adjustment (r=-0.15), Achievement Motivation (r=-0.07) and Emotional Intelligence (r=-0.24). Extraversion was found to have negative association with Adjustment (r=-0.18) and Achievement Motivation (r=-0.10) whereas positive association with Emotional Intelligence (r=0.34). Adjustment was having positive association with Achievement Motivation (r=0.13) and Emotional Intelligence (r=0.10). Achievement Motivation was having positive association with Emotional Intelligence (r=0.20).

The inter correlation of variables reveals that as the neuroticism increases, extraversion, adjustment and achievement motivation also increases. As the extraversion increases, it leads to the enhancement of adjustment, achievement motivation and emotional intelligence. The extraverted individuals are better able to adjust with their family, peer group and society as they have high desire for interpersonal attraction. Likewise highly extraverted individuals have high achievement motivation and are considered to be emotionally intelligent. As the adjustment increases, achievement motivation also increases and emotional intelligence decreases. The highly adjusted adolescents have a strong tendency to motivate themselves and others hence their achievement motivation is also high. Likewise an increase in achievement motivation also leads to increase in emotional intelligence. Because if an individual is self motivated and has high desire for motivating others, he is also able to manage and control his emotions and the emotions of others as well. That is how he becomes emotionally intelligent.

CPSIA information can be obtained
at www.ICGtesting.com
Printed in the USA
LVHW021426011222
734355LV00016B/992

9 781805 452171